Quicksilver Companies

For Anna and Robert Griffiths

This is what we knew at the start
of online – I know you can improve on it

Quicksilver Companies

The battle for the online consumer

by

Alan Griffiths

palgrave

First published 2001 by
PALGRAVE
Houndmills, Basingstoke, Hampshire RG21 6XS and
175 Fifth Avenue, New York, N.Y. 10010
Companies and representatives throughout the world

PALGRAVE is the new global academic imprint of
St. Martin's Press LLC Scholarly and Reference Division and
Palgrave Publishers Ltd (formerly Macmillan Press Ltd).

ISBN 0–333–96028–9 hardcover

This book is printed on paper suitable for recycling and made from fully managed and sustained forest sources.

A catalogue record for this book is available from the British Library.

Library of Congress Cataloging-in-Publication Data has been applied for.

Editing and origination by
Aardvark Editorial, Mendham, Suffolk

10 9 8 7 6 5 4 3 2 1
10 09 08 07 06 05 04 03 02 01

Printed and bound in Great Britain by
Creative Print & Design (Wales), Ebbw Vale

CONTENTS

Contents

LIST OF FIGURES

No one alive has seen anything like the online boom. We have to go back to the time of our great-grandparents to see its like, with the electricity boom of the 1920s. Before that we would have to go back as far as the beginnings of the railways in the 1840s. These represent fundamental changes in the technology which defines and supports the way we live and the way in which we make money. They have common characteristics, for example all of them created a series of booms and busts on the stock market. It turns out that this generation has learnt none of the lessons from long-dead investors about not getting too enthusiastic.

We know we are experiencing another fundamental shift in the way in which the world works. However, I believe that this time it is different.

Online is a very peculiar beast. What is it? It is the ability to communicate via computer (or a computer-like machine) via a universal network. The implications of this are profound. Computers have a phenomenal capàcity to compress and process information. Digital television, which is only in its infancy, is already fast approaching the point where it can deliver thousands of TV programmes direct to your home TV exactly when you want them (and not when a programme scheduler thinks you should want them).

But this is just fairground stuff. The real advantage of a universal computer network connecting every home and business around the world is that information flows unimpeded everywhere. Price fixing, governments being economical with the truth, not knowing that goods that you want are available in other countries and not knowing there is a solution to your work or technology problem – all these fall to the scythe of online. Soon it will be impossible 'not to know'. An unknowing population, who has simply 'not been able to find out', has been the saviour of too many sloppy companies and nasty governments over the last millennium.

The worst offenders are already crumbling; the appalling car service and dealer networks in the UK, travel agents, estate agents and the impossibility of sustaining a dictatorship anywhere in the world in an age of unfettered information.

Online is not just the internet – the internet is simply one form of a universal network (which is why I don't like using 'web' or the 'internet' to describe the phenomenon). There are now many ways of distributing computer-processed information, including television and mobile phones. So 'online' is a good cover-all term to describe businesses or services which use computer networks.

Online is allowing us to live in a completely different way. It means that we can all do more, more quickly. I believe that it has taken off so quickly because a new kind of consumer has emerged who, in order to sustain their lifestyle, would have had to invent this technology had it not existed. This argument is detailed in Chapter 1 and is essential to understanding how to start a successful online venture.

What makes online different from previous technological phenomena is that it produces a step change in what an individual can learn, communicate and action in a single day. This has all sorts of implications. First the velocity of trading is going to accelerate and companies have to be ready for that. Second, we will all become far more productive and therefore wealthier. Goods and services will be available to us that would have been unimaginable even two years ago. A very simple example; last month I managed to sell my house in Kingston-on-Thames over the internet to a Swedish investment banker who would not have normally contemplated living there except that he could see, from Sweden, what good value for money it was compared to better-known areas just two miles away. I now book holiday homes in Florida from Kingston-on-Thames, as the internet allows me to do virtual tours of them from home – I can 'walk' from room to room to see if it meets with the family's approval.

This means that we will all begin to live faster and smarter. Our lives will be more varied and fulfilled because we will know the possibilities that exist in life and we will be able to plan and arrange our lives to realize those possibilities.

I believe that our enjoyment of work will improve, gradually. The impact of online on the workplace is a huge topic which has been barely touched. However, in a book about how to start an online enterprise, it is very pertinent. Retaining the right staff is something which all online entrepreneurs wrestle with, as staff in possession of information about other jobs and employment tend to walk off if they are treated as servants, which is indeed still the way many large organizations treat their staff. People will not be capable of 'being organized' without being told about strategy and goals. Everyone will work hard as long as they believe in what they are working for. If they don't know, or can't guess, they will find somewhere which will give them a reason and appropriate rewards. It will much harder to say 'I hate my job', as it will be far easier to find one which suits you and treats you as a trusted employee. Companies will have no choice. With unfettered information they will have to give you discretion, trust and responsibility if they want to succeed.

All this is the kind of visionary talk about online which can be read elsewhere. The rest of this book is about what, until now, has been shrouded in mystery; how to make an online company work and make money out of it. It is a practical, not a visionary, book about online.

We have just gone through a huge boom and bust wave of online company formation which I believe was the first big wave of online start-ups. The first wave were the pioneers. They experimented, they innovated, and they tried – a few succeeded and many went bust.

This book is designed to create a second wave of online entrepreneurs who can learn from the successes and failures of the first wave. It involves being more disciplined than the first wave, who were often making it up as they went along. It involves using the methods and experience contained in the following chapters to win the battle for the online consumer.

Like the wheel, online will not go away. This is only the beginning. The huge gains lie over the next 20 or 30 years when, probably, another new technology will emerge, even more shocking than online.

But for now those who succeed will be well read in the practical lessons of the first pioneers. That is what this book is about.

I would like to thank everyone who has helped me, knowingly or unknowingly, in the preparation of this book.

First, those who have recounted their companies' experiences, particularly Rupert Howell and Ian Priest of HHCL, who talked about their outstanding work on the branding of Egg; Robin Price for his clear, cool view of cash flow; and Stefan Finch of CD9, who helped with technical information.

Tom Ball, founder of CD9, has been a great influence on my thinking, essentially for demonstrating the true spirit of an online pioneer, pressing on always in the face of any adversity.

I have to thank Stephen Rutt, my editor at Palgrave, for his patience as he received a whole stream of e-mails detailing and revising the book and its deadlines. It is doubtful if the book could have been delivered without the combination of e-mail and Stephen.

I am indebted to Doug Richardson for his thinking on branding, my colleague Martin Roche for his incisive and often devastating analysis of business triumphs and failures, and Mark Smith for his good-humoured common sense about business start-ups. Most of all, I am indebted to Roger Woods for rescuing me from the clutches of the BBC.

Tim Bell (now Lord Bell of Belgravia) has been mainly responsible for this book appearing as he thought that my ideas about online were sufficiently interesting three years ago to provide me with stimulating and varied employment as an 'online consultant', although neither of us at the time quite knew what the job entailed. Through this indulgence he has been responsible for the experimentation, vision and time needed to produce the ideas and methods which appear in these pages.

Finally, my wife Gill constantly contributes to my thinking about the new economy by reminding me that, as a result of selling the house over the internet, we now have a new one to redecorate. It is a strong reminder that, despite the power of online, the problems of living in a pile of bricks and mortar will probably always be with us.

ALAN GRIFFITHS
Kingston Gate
New Year's Day 2001

Every effort has been made to trace all the copyright holders but if any have been inadvertently overlooked the publishers will be pleased to make the necessary arrangements at the first opportunity.

The Knowledge

The greatest thrill of working in electronic commerce is that you know that it is different. Whatever line of e-commerce you start in, you can be sure that almost no one has ever done it before. You are not standing on giant's shoulders, because in this land no one has walked, big or small, until your feet touched this ground and laid claim to this soil.

With this feeling comes the reality of what it must have been like to have been a pioneer of the first Industrial Revolution. Setting up shop in the north of England in the mid-18th century, well away from the change-resisting guilds of the south, with a mill full of strangely named devices such as 'spinning jennies' or 'mules'. Being considered strange and unnatural by your old-fashioned competitors. Enduring scepticism and ridicule about what you had spent and the risks you had taken. Until the orders came in, the market changed, your competitors weakened and you started to make a large profit.

Above all, the early mill owners must have coped with what the new economy entrepreneurs are discovering today: complete uncertainty and perpetual change. Not knowing if the system will work – and not knowing if anyone will buy what they have to sell. Most importantly, not knowing whether your cash will run out before profitability dawns.

As in the first Industrial Revolution, the new economy companies are like quicksilver – they can make you very rich – or you can be sucked cashless into them. In order to survive, these companies have to adapt and constantly listen to what the market wants. The new economy companies, the online companies, are quicksilver companies. They change shape, adapt, transform the world or eat their owners – 'a terrible beauty is born'.

This book is based on the reality of online commerce. Unlike the books which have gone before, hyping it, speculating about it or promoting it, there is now enough experience of online start-ups and failures to at last talk about that rare and precious asset, knowledge. What to do, when to do it, how to plan your business and the risks to avoid.

So this book is about how to win at online commerce. It is not about how it will all end, and who will ultimately win. It is based on what we know now about who is winning and why, and what we can learn as we look back over e-commerce's short history. It is about the reality of e-commerce and the lessons we have learnt so far.

The online checklist

To make this book more useful to any reader high on ambition and short on time, each chapter represents one or two ticks in a checklist to test the value of an online idea.

If your idea for an online company can successfully complete every point in this checklist, it will, according to what we know about online success at the start of the year 2001, stand an excellent chance of being outstandingly successful. But a warning: it won't. Every online business contains flaws – things that will force it to concede a tick or two as you progress a business idea through this book. It is simply that their positive points are so positive that they outweigh the negatives. The twelfth chapter of the book, 'How to Use It All', tests some real online companies against the checklist and sees how and why they are successful and demonstrates how important it is to have some very positive points, as opposed to an average score throughout.

Here is a summary of the hurdles your online idea will have to clear to be viable in the new economy. Each hurdle is dealt with in detail in each chapter.

1   Quicksilver

The modern consumer has changed significantly since the mid-1990s. They now have a set of demands and needs which mean that if online technology hadn't existed it would have had to have been invented.

In order to prosper from the unreasonable demands of this new consumer your business idea will have to be 'new consumer' friendly. Otherwise it will probably not thrive online as the new consumer is far and away the biggest adopter of the new technology.

2   Supply chain reactions

Much online business succeeds by capturing a vulnerable part of a supply chain. A complete chain, one which runs all the way from the maker of the smallest rivet to the consumer who buys the finished product at the other end, is known as a 'supply chain'. Successful online businesses sit across the supply chain at the part where the greatest profit exists, rather like fishing in a river at the point where all the fattest fish swim closest to the surface.

This chapter allows you to think of your market as a supply chain and to check you are across the most profitable part of it.

3   The technology test

Is your business idea really an online idea? It seems a daft question but many rush into the new economy with an idea which could easily be done conventionally. Is any extra value being added by being online? If not, your idea is not a new technology idea. It is doubtful, for example, if most current retail businesses should be online, which also explains why they are struggling to demonstrate extra profitability to shareholders.

4   Timing

Two things bedevil online ideas; they can be either ahead of the *market* or ahead of the *technology*. Either means that they will not enjoy anything like the anticipated level of sales.

This chapter tells you how to determine if the market or the technology is there to support your online idea.

5   Defining the market

As most online business ideas are entirely new, it is possible to use them to define entirely new markets. For example, Amazon.com is the world leader in the online book market, a market which didn't exist before Amazon.com created it.

This chapter examines whether you can use your idea to define a market which your business can lead. An important issue is whether that market can or will exist. The chapter suggests how to test whether certain online markets are viable or not.

6 Online branding

Some products are seemingly immortal, such as Coca-Cola and Mars. This is because they have created emotional reasons for consumers to believe in them and to want to keep buying them. This process is called branding.

Online products can be branded and promoted in many new ways made possible by computer technology. This chapter suggests ways of doing this, so that your online brand can be more powerful than any traditional brand which has preceded it.

7 The plan and the pitch

You need a plan to be able to pitch your business to potential backers and consumers. But great ideas can be ruined by mediocre plans. Great plans have thought of all the important aspects of the business and how your management will tackle them.

However, great plans can also be ruined by mediocre presentation. This chapter looks at how to present a plan of an online venture, what to emphasize in it and how to make it come alive for your audience.

8 Doing the numbers

This deals with the financial side of the business – what are the important financial figures to watch, and how investors will measure the performance of an online business, once it is up and running.

Online businesses have new assets which are not accurately captured by conventional accounting methods but which are critical in determining the value of your online business. This chapter tells you what these are and how to account for them, in order to work out how much your business is currently worth.

9 Partnerships

Like all the best marriages finding the right partner in the first place translates into wealth, health and happiness. Venture capitalists, or banks, can be troublesome bedfellows – tossing and turning when what you need is calm. The best partner is often one who brings something to your venture that you need but don't have, for example marketing expertise.

This chapter takes the form of a number of case studies of partnerships which do and don't work and suggests the best way to find the ideal backer.

10 The where

The location of online enterprises is becoming a critical issue. This is because both the content and transactions of an online service can be placed in any location, regardless of the countries in which it is received.

This has profound implications for both the tax paid by your company and the regulatory regime under which it falls. This chapter examines where and how you should set up the physical location of your business and whether you should divide it between several different places to maximize the advantages.

11 The team

Unless you have the right people, your idea will remain grounded. This chapter deals with the best way to structure an online business, where to find the people to run it and how to reward them when they are working for you.

12 How to use it all

This is a review of all the methods and checkpoints in the book so far, with some examples of how real companies have taken advantage of successful online tactics.

This chapter looks at what to watch when an online business is actually up and running and what ultimately building an online business is about.

13 Product checks

The most important and regular series of checks you should carry out when your business is up and running are; *do your products do what your business says they do?*

This chapter allows you to check that your business is delivering the goods, using online and offline technology.

14 Where is it all going?

The book assumes that you have had an online idea and want to use the experiences of the first wave of online entrepreneurs to create and run your business to build on their successes and not their mistakes. That way you will become part of the second wave, the tried and trusted foundations of the online economy.

This chapter looks at some of the markets which, if your idea is not quite yet fixed in concrete, you ought to aim at if you want to ride the areas of the online economy which are likely to grow in the next five years.

Quicksilver Companies

Quicksilver Companies allows you to test your online idea against what we now know about online success and failure. It will allow you to change your plans, or refine them. In the end, the risk will be yours, but a little knowledge based on others' experience of this fast-moving world will be a very powerful and competitive weapon.

CHAPTER 1

Quicksilver

No new technology, however clever, can or will be adopted unless there is a ready and eager market for it. The history of many inventions, consequently, is that they languish for many years before becoming commercial.

When Thomas Edison first demonstrated the phonograph to the US President in 1880, he described it as a 'dictation machine'. He didn't realize he'd just invented the technology behind a billion-dollar recording industry because consumers did not demand records. But within 40 years recording became a boom industry.

However, the striking thing about online technology, and in particular the internet, is the rapidity with which it was taken up. The graph in Figure 1.1 is a modern classic, probably the first graph to achieve iconographic status. I first saw it in a presentation written by MacKinsey for the BBC in 1996 but its origins are earlier than that and it featured in analysts' reports as early as 1994.

It shows the speed of adoption of the internet compared to three other new electronic media in North America, radio, TV and cable. It shows, quite simply, the internet outpacing them all by several leagues.

This graph made decision makers aware that the internet was being adopted significantly faster than either radio and TV had been and convinced them that this was the next boom medium (and the one to make them money very fast, the ultimate quicksilver generator).

But why was the consumer suddenly clamouring for the internet, something which in 1990 hardly anyone had heard of?

In the gold rush which followed, most creators of online businesses failed to ask this question. But it is a crucial question, as the answer to it determines whether your online business will fly or crash. If your online idea addresses the demands of the voracious adopters of the internet, it will have a ready audience. If it doesn't, it will stall.

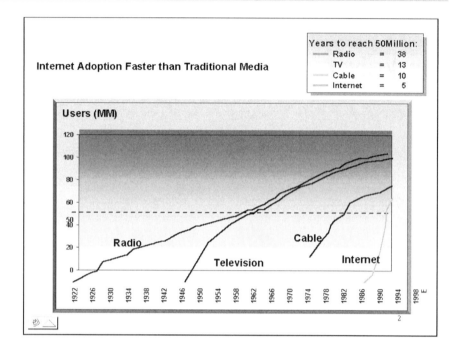

Figure 1.1 Internet adoption faster than traditional media

What created the internet boom?

The fact is that in the 1990s workers in developed countries began to go through a fundamental change, involving their attitudes, lifestyles, outlook and, most importantly, the way in which they worked and lived. And that is what has brought about the online revolution more than anything else. There is a profound debate about whether technology produces social change (as Marx believed) or whether social changes demand the technology to enable change to occur. In the case of the latest twist in the online revolution, it is the latter. Technological change has been stimulated and accelerated by a fundamental social change, which has created the insatiable appetite we experience today for online commerce.

In order to succeed in e-commerce, you have to understand the nature of that change, because to succeed you have to exploit it. It is hard to describe but it is most easily summed up by a simple idea – the death of choice.

The death of choice

Choice was the biggest dynamic of the consumer society of the twentieth century. It was only in the 1990s that it began to die.

Choice is not the first or necessary product of mass production. Henry Ford's Detroit production lines resulted in a car which was affordable and which could be adapted to many tasks. However, it was essentially always the same car (the model T) and it was always black.

But in the mid-1920s, Ford's competitors started to think of ways to compete against Ford and his massive share of the car market. A remarkable man called Alfred Pierpoint Sloan was appointed President of General Motors and he started to listen to the desires, rather than the immediate needs, of the car consumer. In doing so he created the first model ranges where there were several cars, each more expensive and more powerful than the last. The basic idea was that, rather than offer everyone the same car (as Ford did), General Motors would offer a range through which buyers could migrate as they became more affluent and aspirational.

So consumers gained a choice. Sloan extended this so that there was even choice among versions of the same model – migrating from standard to luxury to deluxe. The idea was to hook the consumer by allowing them a limited choice – but one which was significant enough to enable them to distinguish themselves from the Joneses, or the worker a grade below them in the company car park.

This version of product marketing became so powerful and has been with us for so long that many companies still find it hard to think in any other way, even today. But it has significant weaknesses, which should be obvious to anyone starting up a new economy company.

The first is that it relies on buyers behaving like sheep, that is, large groups of people who behave similarly and choose the same product. That is the logic of mass production and product ranges. With a mass of people buying the same product, it is also possible to describe these groups according to the products they buy. Newspapers love the challenge. Consequently, you get 'Mondeo man', 'Capri drivers' or 'Range Rovers'.

Similarly, television was originally only possible as a mass-produced medium. There were a limited number of terrestrial channels. Consequently it was useful to herd people together into ABC or NBC watchers. They had a choice, but the choice was a compromise. The weakness of this model is demonstrated by the comment which people often make about television channels that 'there is nothing on'. What they mean is that there is plenty on but nothing of interest exactly for them. Channels are a compromise, they offer choice, but a very limited one.

Choice among product ranges is a compromise. It works as long as large groups of people are *not* affluent enough to buy the car or product which is built exactly for them. You buy a Mondeo or a Mustang, not the car which is exactly right for you. Product ranges are a convenient veil over the homogeneity of mass production, which makes things affordable through compromise and thinking of people as sheep.

But two things started to happen to employees in the 1990s which meant that choice was no longer enough:

- People became more *affluent*

- People's *time* started to become very precious.

These are the two most important aspects of the new online consumer. Everything else follows as a consequence of them. Any new online business has to take into account both what has caused them to happen and how they affect online trading.

So why has the new consumer emerged and why has it happened so suddenly?

The quicksilver consumer

It is almost certain that the modern consumer, this strange beast who emerged in the mid-1990s, is a result of the 1980s' telecommunications revolution. 'Almost' certain because very little research has been done on this phenomenon, although its consequences are everywhere to be seen. The impact of the modern consumer involves the sudden rise of the internet – the fastest growing medium in history – and also the spectacular decline of mass-market retailers, such as Marks & Spencer, and almost any form of scheduled television channel. Scheduled television channels deny this but ask them for a direct answer to the question: 'what has your gross number of viewers being doing for the last four years?' The true answer, if you can get it, is: 'steadily declining'.

The 1980s' telecommunications revolution consisted of two elements:

- The laying of high-capacity fibre optic backbones around the world

- The deregulation of telecommunications companies.

The second of these was almost more important than the first. It meant that competition arrived on the doorstep of comfortable monopolies such as AT&T and British Telecom, which resulted in a lot of investment in capacity and a falling price of worldwide communications. Suddenly it was affordable both to talk to and exchange data between London and Los Angeles and a lot of other places besides.

This had one very strange effect. It meant that the general prediction of the early 1980s, that the new technology would give us all more time, went into reverse. In both America and Europe, pundits in newspapers had predicted that by the year 2000 we would all have so much leisure time, due to computerization, that we would have difficulty in working out what to do with it all. Golf courses would be packed, holiday islands full to bursting.

However, the opposite happened, for the simple reason that London was now competing directly with Los Angeles as well as New York and Tokyo. The telecommunications companies had now made it feasible to select your consultancy, insurance and financial services from thousands of miles away. These industries, rapidly followed by others, suddenly found that they were competing with the best worldwide. This had two effects:

- Their employees had to work harder and longer to compete with the best in the world

- Individuals in these industries became richer, as they were now competing with the best of world class and not merely the best of national class. People who are best in the world get paid more as employers worldwide know about them and can bid for their services.

So service sector workers in particular suddenly found themselves richer, but with no spare time. And this phenomenon spread as more industries sought to define themselves as *service industries*, because the profit margins were better in the service sector rather than in manufacturing. For example, car makers started to concentrate on financing your transport requirements, rather than selling cars directly to you.

All of this has had a profound impact on consumer habits. Consumers are suddenly affluent and short of time. This makes choice unappetizing as far as they are concerned. They do not want:

- A range of goods between which they have to choose, as this takes time

- A set of goods which identifies them as part of a tribe. They are affluent and feel that they belong to no group but are simply a unique, affluent individual

- Anything mass produced. It is not specific enough to their needs.

There has been a lot of agonizing in the press about why mass-production retailers such as Marks & Spencer (and latterly Gap) are doing so badly.

John Jay, a *Sunday Times* columnist, writes that 'some investors have all but given up on the chain, arguing that its success was a mere accident of the times and that it is destined for a permanent spiral of decline'.[1]

Those investors are absolutely right. Marks & Spencer's problem is that it is known for manufacturing ranges of high-quality, affordable clothes. This was very laudable before the 1990s. But the present-day consumer no longer wants mass-produced ranges, they want *exactly what they want when they want it*. If they don't get it, they migrate to a company who is prepared to give it to them. They may not find this company quickly but they will keep on trying until they do. That is why retailers in particular are now experiencing such promiscuity among consumers and finding it hard to lock onto their tastes and desires, as they try to return to the safe methods of mass production and categorize them.

Here are some phrases which the respected consumer research body The Henley Centre uses to categorize the quicksilver consumer:

> Consumers are now ... demanding the right to choose a price that is right for them.

> People now actively seek to minimize time wastage, turning 'bad' time into 'good'. A feeling of control over the structure of time is at the very heart of our sense of well-being.

> The consumer is now in control of markets, with rapidly increasing spending power and confidence. Companies do not tell consumers what to do today, they have to listen for instructions.[2]

This means that companies which are known for handing down product ranges they think the customer ought to choose from are now dead. Marks & Spencer is dead, and, long term, so is scheduled television, including ABC, NBC, ITV. They might evolve into something else but relying on pushing scheduled programmes at an ever-increasing group of people who want *exactly what they want when they want it* is commercial suicide.

The reasonable reader may think that the quicksilver consumer is unreasonable; however, consider the types of job in which the quicksilver consumer works. These jobs are in services, and tend to be computer assisted and client driven. If their client does not get exactly what he or she wants when they want it, they know that client will walk away. They experience it at work and when they come to shop themselves they expect immediate service from the people who are selling to them.

Satisfying the quicksilver consumer

So which companies are succeeding with this new consumer and how are they doing it? The answer is simply any company, online or offline, which gives the new consumer *exactly what they want when they want it*. In this lies a simple truth – it is possible to do this now without computer technology but eventually the demands of the new consumer will become so unreasonable that it will only be possible to operate efficiently by using computer technology.

However, some offline companies do get close to it – primarily those where using the product in some way necessarily constrains the demands of the consumer. Hotels are a good example. To consume the services of a hotel you have to be in one, so the time that visitors stay in a hotel is exploited by enlightened hotel companies. All the top hotels now compete on knowing their customers' likes and dislikes and trying to remember them (not always successfully). The idea is to anticipate each customer's needs and give them what they want before they think of it (which is almost *before* they want it).

Airlines are another such service. To consume the product you have to sit in the same place for long periods; you don't have much of a choice. Branson's Virgin, although it has stumbled in some of its other activities, has always been good at giving the new consumer exactly what they want when they want it in an aircraft. He worked out early on that the new consumer no longer even wanted to go to Spain but was prepared to go all the way to Miami or Orlando, as long as the children were distracted by high tech video equipment and games. So Branson went all out to install it on his planes. But it was a struggle:

> We wanted to borrow $20 million to put new video equipment in the planes, but we were turned down. So we got on to Boeing and said if we buy some 747-400s will you throw in a fourteen channel video? They said, yes. It was the same with Airbus. The bizarre thing in life is you can't borrow $20 million for new video systems, but you can borrow $2 billion for new planes.[3]

The lesson here is an important one. Branson was prepared to borrow heavily to install video and games on demand in his aircraft as he realized he couldn't satisfy modern consumers without the technology. Although his airline isn't exactly an online service, it is already relying heavily on online technology to meet the demands of the quicksilver consumer.

Online quicksilver

However, the reason the internet took off so quickly is that it is almost the perfect technology with which to satisfy the new consumer. It allows, in theory, a cornucopia of products, with buyers and sellers worldwide meeting on one medium. Eventually it will be hard to say that you can't find exactly what you want when you want it. The barrier is the tools which allow you to do this. It has been argued, with justification, that the problem with the internet is that it will find a screwdriver for you but is unable to distinguish whether you were after a tool, a cocktail or a porn service. Context and grammar are not its strengths.

However, the tools are becoming ever-more refined and the most promising avenue is the kind of tool which plays the 'top hotel trick', allowing you to know so much about the individual wandering around your online premises that you can tell him or her what they want before they want it. This is a transitional technology, but for now captures, as well as the present technology can, what drives the new consumer. This technology is known by the portmanteau phrase of 'personalization'. By and large, sites which offer personalization do well, as they deal with the quicksilver consumer in a way which they like and understand.

Take www.napster.com, a Californian site which allows people to swap digital music tracks. Napster hit the news because its users simply swop tracks again and again, making rather a nonsense of the music industry's business model. It has acquired 38 million users in its first year, making it the fastest growing website of all time (Figure 1.2).

A cynic would say that it owes its growth to the simple fact that users can download music for free. But there are other sites which do this. What Napster managed to do was combine free downloads (or swaps) with a high degree of personalization.

On the Napster software (which users download) everyone is given a personal portfolio which they can use to trade or talk about music. Essentially it is a form of personalization which allows music fans to behave as a community, doing what they want when they want in the way they want. It is this facility to which Napster owes its growth, not primarily to the free downloads.

Another website (for an older demographic) which owes its appeal to personalization is Interactive Investor International (www.iii.co.uk). This allows investors to build up a portfolio where the value of their shares is updated every 15 minutes using a feed from the relevant stock exchange. The portfolio page is entirely personal to the user (Figure 1.3). Before online technology this was almost impossible to do and involved compli-

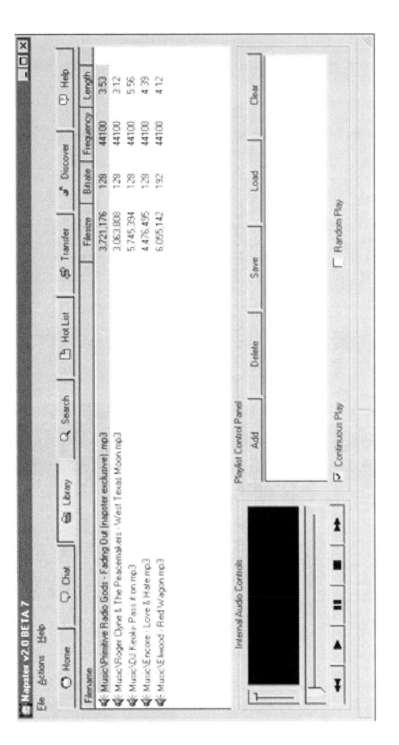

Figure 1.2 A personal portfolio of songs ready to roll on Napster software

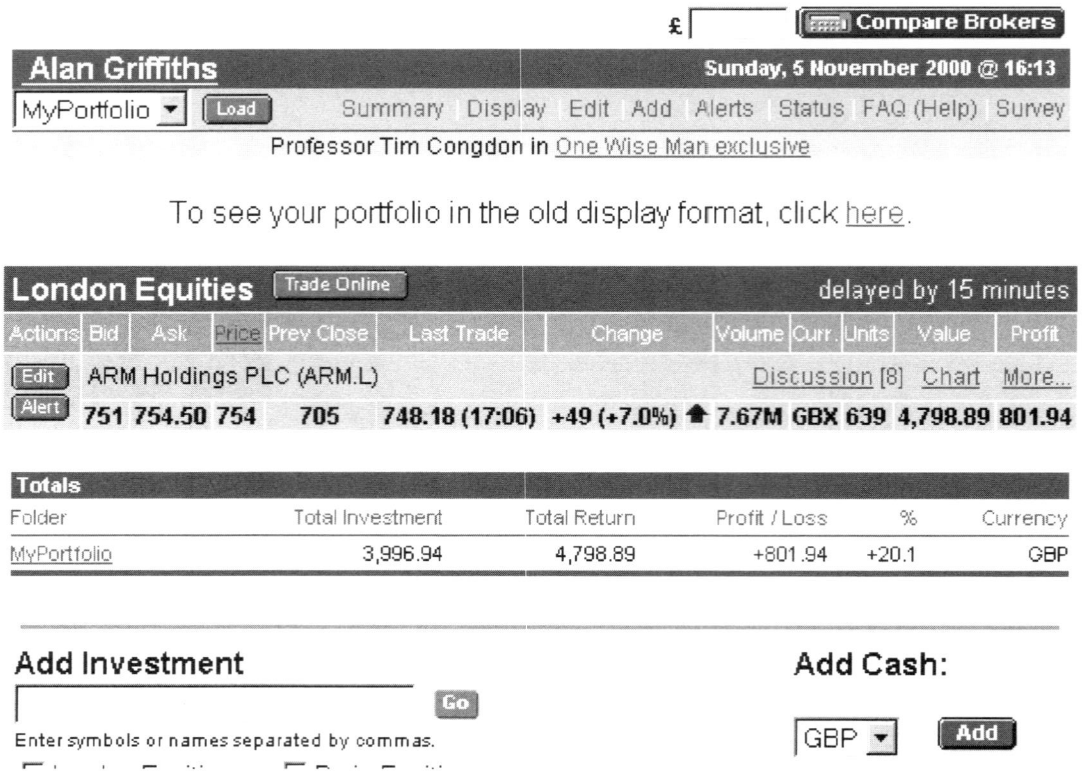

Alan Griffiths

[MyPortfolio ▼] [Load]   Summary Display Edit Add Alerts Status FAQ (Help) Survey

Sunday, 5 November 2000 @ 16:13

Professor Tim Congdon in One Wise Man exclusive

To see your portfolio in the old display format, click here.

London Equities [Trade Online]

delayed by 15 minutes

Actions	Bid	Ask	Price	Prev Close	Last Trade	Change	Volume	Cur.	Units	Value	Profit
			ARM Holdings PLC (ARM.L)					Discussion [8]	Chart	More...
[Edit]											
[Alert]	751	754.50	754	705	748.18 (17:06)	+49 (+7.0%) ⬆	7.67M	GBX	639	4,798.89	801.94

Totals

Folder	Total Investment	Total Return	Profit / Loss	%	Currency
MyPortfolio	3,996.94	4,798.89	+801.94	+20.1	GBP

Add Investment

[   ] [Go]

Enter symbols or names separated by commas.

Add Cash:

[GBP ▼] [Add]

Figure 1.3 A personal portfolio in Interactive Investor International

cated links between pieces of software on your computer and data feeds. The power of this model is that it gives the shareholder exactly what they want when they want it – no more and no less.

However, as online develops it will be possible to get even closer to the individual user (some of the later chapters explore this in more depth). But the most important point is that online has been grasped because the consumer no longer wants to be grouped, massed or compromised. And computer technology can deliver that to them. This is the heart of the quicksilver boom.

CHECKPOINTS

■ Can you save your users time compared with how they obtained goods and services in the past?

■ Does your online business idea allow you to deliver exactly what the new consumer wants when they want it?

CHAPTER 2

Supply Chain Reactions

One of the most irritating moments of being a television director is when, as you wrestle with the script, the shots and getting the show to end exactly on time, Engineering rings up and tells you not a single picture you are sending is going out. Normally at this point someone shouts: 'It was OK leaving us!' This phrase has become, in a way, the epitaph of once great television organizations such as the BBC. Quite simply, they failed to appreciate that anything really mattered after a signal left the studio. The mysterious chain which linked the studio with the viewer was inhabited by a jungle of lines, masts and transmission faults. *It was OK leaving us*, so everything was basically all right.

Except that it wasn't. Down that chain lurked a series of deadly, unseen predators who moved into its dark corners and started to gnaw away at the BBC's hold over its viewers. They had spotted something that, too late, the BBC woke up to – there was another link in its supply chain with the end-user which digital technology would lay bare.

Supply chains are the steps which link the supplier of the smallest component to the final buyer of the finished product. Analysing them is not new. However, online has changed the shape of them for many industries. Close, established relationships have been disrupted by them. Venerable old organizations have woken up to find that companies which apparently had nothing to do with their market, such as Microsoft, are now their biggest competitor.

Supply chain analysis is essential, as your online company may not be trading at the most profitable part of that supply chain. For example, you may be at the end of the chain, trading 'business to consumer' (B2C) when the most profitable part of that chain is in fact further up at the 'business to business' (B2B) end. Determining the most profitable part is tricky, however, as an attack by online operators on a supply chain may change its dynamics. That is why I firmly believe that going first in online business is a very risky business. It is far better to be second and reap the benefits of others' experience, while third is too late.

Defining the chain

Most chains come in a simple four-stage model (Figure 2.1). This is applied to manufactured products and it is easy to see how they fit into this template. However, most online businesses are service businesses, often selling intangible goods such as television pictures or ideas. This sometimes extends the model or changes the stages in the chain. The easiest way to show this is to take an example such as television, which will also show how the BBC managed to miss a vital link in its supply chain.

The television model (Figure 2.2) consists of five stages. They are fairly obvious; ideas and scripts are turned into television programmes which are packaged as part of a channel and then pumped out through the transmitter network. This is the old, restricted world of terrestrial television where there are only four or five channels because there is limited spectrum space in which to transmit them.

However, apply digital technology to this chain and its dynamics change completely. The fourth box, transmission, goes up for grabs

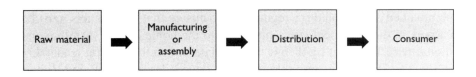

Figure 2.1 A typical supply chain

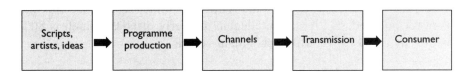

Figure 2.2 The television supply chain

because online allows many new ways of distributing television – notably via satellite with unlimited spectrum space. This has happened with a vengeance in Europe and is creating a complete shift in the balance of broadcasting power. It will not be long before the US succumbs to the same revolution.

The BBC failed to understand that this last link in the chain is now vital to the dominance of the television supply chain as it commanded a direct relationship with the viewer (the consumer). In the early 1990s, television executives thought that people would not want more television channels and therefore the way in which they were sent to the viewer was irrelevant.

They were wrong. They failed to understand three things:

- The demand for niche channels, which met the increasingly diverse needs and affluence of the TV audience, was big and powerful, meaning that many more television channels could be sustained

- The most profitable, powerful part of the supply chain was ultimately the part where viewers had to subscribe in order to receive these channels

- The technology in effect formed an electronic 'gateway' which could potentially prevent programme and channel makers from reaching viewers.

So suddenly it was not OK if 'it was OK leaving us', because none of the subsequent parts of the supply chain could be taken for granted. The BBC complained and lobbied for regulations to ensure that its channels must be carried on the new electronic conduits into the home – cable, satellite and digital terrestrial. But by then it was too late, it had lost market leadership of the new UK television world and had conceded it to BSkyB and Rupert Murdoch, who had gone to great lengths to develop digital technology in order to link the viewer to a plethora of television channels.

The digital satellite set-top box software and architecture are closely guarded. The most important component is the conditional access system which tells the channel management system which channels and pay per view programmes a viewer has paid for and is entitled to watch. This code is never released, as it is the intellectual property of NDS, which is 80% owned by News Corp., Murdoch's main vehicle.

The fat part of the chain

Why did News Corp. go to such lengths to guard its direct relationship with the television subscriber? The answer is because it was potentially the most profitable part of this online chain. Rather like supermarket retailing, the best place to be is in direct contact with the consumer where, although no one product is worth much, the overall number of consumers creates substantial revenues.

There are those who argue that the best place to be in the digital television chain is in programme production as, with so many channels, they will outbid each other for the best content. To a certain extent this is true, and has certainly made English football and American basketball clubs rich. However, ultimately it is false, because, as tastes change and new viewers emerge, the gatekeeper at the end of the chain will have the first opportunity to respond to new tastes and commission new programmes of their own. So digital broadcasters can become the masters of content production as well. The direct relationship with the end-user in the television chain dominates it in the same way that knowing what shoppers are buying helps supermarkets to dominate their supply chain.

The BBC's problem is that it is stuck down the chain in channel management and television production and has little direct contact with its viewers. Unless it evolves this, it will increasingly be marginalized by competitors who do have direct contact.

However, the biggest profits are not always to be found at the end of a supply chain. For example, the supply chain for the automotive industry holds some surprises (Figure 2.3).

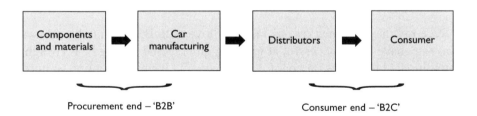

Figure 2.3 Supply chain for the automotive industry

Surely the best place to set up an online operation in the automotive chain would be between the consumer and the manufacturer (and so take share from the traditional retailers). But this has proved very tricky for the dot.coms. The reason is that the gross profit available to be shared out among automotive distributors is heavily fought over. There is overcapacity in the car market, margins are low and, in the UK, volume and prices are decreasing as more and more people buy from abroad.

This highly competitive market puts heavy pressure on manufacturers to cut costs. One way of doing this is online procurement, which allows companies to shop for components from more manufacturers, which in turn reduces prices as they all compete for the business. It also eliminates a lot of paperwork that goes backwards and forwards in any procurement process and thus reduces costs.

Online procurement companies have been doing extremely well in markets where the sales to the end-user are either highly competitive or highly regulated (so reducing the gross profit at the end of the supply chain). In effect, these online ventures have found that trading further up the chain (at the procurement end) produces a higher gross return.

The mathematics of this is very simple:

Gross profit = Profit margin × Price of a product × Volume of sales

In the supply chain, your online business venture should be sitting across the part which has the greatest volume, the highest prices and the biggest volume of sales. In the car industry this is at the procurement end.

B2B or B2C?

Recently the stock market has fallen in love with B2B online businesses, as they have been successful at growing quickly and getting heavyweight, traditional businesses on board. Less successful have been online ventures at the consumer end of the chain, the B2C businesses.

It is not clear why B2B has managed to establish itself faster than B2C, although there are three likely reasons:

▩ Competition

▩ History

▩ Fear.

Competition is the simple explanation; all the industries which have adopted online procurement in a big way have intense competition at the consumer end and so are eager to lower their manufacturing costs. However, this is an unsatisfactory explanation, as these procurement systems are being set up as joint ventures between highly competitive industry rivals.

For example, California-based CommerceOne is one of the most successful online procurement providers in the world. It has managed to persuade the automotive, oil and aerospace industries all to set up joint procurement systems. This means that in practice DaimlerChrysler, Ford and General Motors have a joint venture company to procure components and materials from their suppliers online. The argument is that the bigger and more transparent the market for suppliers the keener the price of components.

What is baffling about this is that it confers no apparent competitive advantage on any of the companies involved. It may create a very large market but as knowledge of suppliers and their prices is equally accessible to all parties then presumably they will all get equal supply advantages from the system. It increases the gap between those on the system and those struggling with conventional procurement but in effect creates a buying cartel, something which the competition authorities investigated before allowing the venture to go ahead.

The same type of procurement system is being established in the oil industry where Texaco, BP Amoco and Shell have also joined in a CommerceOne venture.

The effect on CommerceOne's growth has been exceptional. CommerceOne works by taking a small part of the value of every deal which its system processes. It estimated that, with these three large joint ventures, by the end of the year 2000 it would have $1 trillion of revenue going through CommerceOne. By this measure B2B is the place to be.

History is the second factor which may explain why such large companies rush headlong into B2B without pausing to ask why it makes them more competitive.

The history of the previous Industrial Revolution (in the early 19th century) shows that in certain industries B2B revenues grew faster and lasted longer than B2C revenues. The reason for this is that competition was eventually so fierce at the consumer end of the supply chain that hardly any B2C companies made a profit. The following case study on the growth of the railways in the UK illustrates how B2B was better than B2C when this early example of a high tech industry grew in the 1840s.

Is the dot.com crash a rail crash?

Nicholas Craft, at the London School of Economics, has done a fascinating analysis of the 1845 slump in rail shares. It is an excellent lesson in how B2B trade was more profitable than B2C trade, and it also shows how the stock market did not distinguish between the two (as it also fails to do today).

Between the end of 1845 and the middle of 1848, for example, shares in Great Western Railway (running between London and the West) slumped by 56%, which was not as sudden or deep as those of QXL.com (about 90% in 2000) but still a sure-fire way to lose money. The good news for those looking for modern parallels is that subsequently revenues from railways increased by 470% over the next 20 years. The stock market had initially understood that railways were new, different and would have an impact on the UK economy and they were right.

However, they were right in the wrong way. Most investors in 1845 assumed that railways would make most of their money from moving people (a B2C proposition). In fact, the largest proportion of railway revenues eventually came from moving freight, particularly the minerals needed by Victorian industry. Thus railways became much more important as a B2B proposition than a B2C one. Similarly in the dot.com market, we find that e-procurement platforms, which speed up businesses buying materials from suppliers (such as CommerceOne or Ariba), are steaming ahead and sites which let you auction a railway ticket to a punter are struggling.

But, you ask, as dot.com managements constantly assure us that they are moving closer to profitability – *were the railways ever profitable*? I'm afraid the answer is 'not very and hardly ever', which is unbelievable, given that by 1870 half a billion pounds had been spent constructing them. The reason for this was that everyone jumped onto the railway bandwagon (does this sound disturbingly familiar?) and, as a result, there were too many lines. One of the last to be built, Grand Central, never paid a dividend. Also it appears that the railway pioneers struggled to control costs. It sounds as though Isambard Kingdom Brunel (builder of the Great Western) and Boo.com have more in common than he could possibly have imagined.

However, it was not all gloom. Competition was so fierce that it was the users of the railways, not the shareholders, who gained the most. The price of moving freight and the price of travel fell massively – the cost of going a mile went from 6.5 pence to 1.35 pence. So what shareholders lost the consumer gained – very similar to the price of PCs today.

However, *railways are not information technology*. The important point about information technology is that it makes you fiercely productive. So did railways – a bit. If you take the whole impact of the railways on the UK's wealth over 50 years (1850–1900) it increased economic growth by 0.1%. But in the US, information technology and the internet has already increased growth by four times that in just 3 years.

In the end you have to ask 'does it make us all wealthier?' In the case of the railways, the answer seems to have been 'hardly' and in the case of information technology 'very'. So think how much you can get done on your laptop next time you are stuck on the Great Western Line.

The problem with this explanation is that it is unlikely that modern internet companies are guided by the history of the nineteenth century.

The real reason that B2B trade has grown so fast, and sucked so many traditional companies into its clutches, is probably fear – a fear generated through ignorance. Companies find their supply chain ambushed and panic. In fact the way to get rich in online ventures is to exploit ignorance through an ambush.

Ambushing a supply chain

In 1997 it was very difficult indeed to persuade established European companies that they should have any kind of online strategy. Presentations were met with polite incredulity. Then, in early 2000, things changed, and not merely because of the appreciation of dot.com stocks. Fundamentally it was that traditional businesses found that their relationship with the consumer, and with their suppliers, was being threatened by well-funded online bandits.

These bandits were taking a risk, but they were striking in force and striking in the most unlikely places. Take the heavy equipment industry, not the most obvious place for online invaders. However, in 2000 a whole host of online companies targeted old heavy equipment manufacturers (Figure 2.4). Venerable brands such as Caterpillar and Komatsu suddenly found themselves competing with Californian dot.coms with names like IronPlanet.com and Cephren.com[1].

Wall Street had decided that the heavy equipment industry was ripe for a shake-up and attacked its supply chain where it sold to the consumer; in this case construction and hire companies. The financiers clearly believed

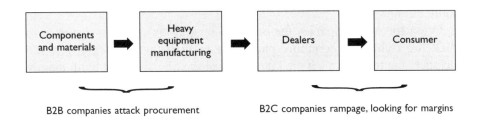

B2B companies attack procurement   B2C companies rampage, looking for margins

Figure 2.4 The online invaders ambush the heavy equipment market

that high ticket price items such as diggers and tractors would be much cheaper to sell online than through traditional dealer networks. Worse was to follow. Some procurement platforms persuaded a few manufacturers to start buying supplies online through their new internet systems. Any heavy digger maker left out of this rush started to panic.

Komatsu and Caterpillar were the first to react, in the middle of 2000, and formed an alliance with one of the B2C invaders, IronPlanet. It is unlikely that either company asked whether this gave them a competitive advantage. It is likely that the main reason they did it was fear – these newcomers were having a detrimental effect on their share price and they had to react.

Fear is a great spur and can give online invaders substance, whether they have attacked the right industry at its fattest point or not (and whether or not they have the revenue). The reaction of the established players is a major irrationality in online planning and unfortunately cannot be predicted.

IronPlanet is now surfing along on the reputation of Komatsu and Caterpillar, who have invested in it substantially. They have both announced e-business initiatives. Caterpillar has launched a new systems and processes division which will concentrate on integrating manufacturing with customer needs. In other words, it has created a defensive online shield all the way up its supply chain.

However, it is not over yet. Other online invaders left without a heavy equipment partner are repositioning themselves to see if there are other ways of attracting the online buyer. Cephren has merged with Bidcom, renamed itself Citadon, and now offers project management services.

All this illustrates that once a supply chain is attacked the threat rarely goes away. Caterpillar's response has been to try and create an online proposition which goes all the way up the supply chain, in order to deter the invaders. But this is expensive and overextends Caterpillar. It didn't do everything in the old world, so why should it be good at doing everything online?

Often for old companies the only response to an online invasion is to pick the right new economy partners and pick them quickly. For the invaders the trick is to get the fattest part of the line and hit it hard, mainly with publicity that they are very much in town.

Second is best

The consultants of the late 1990s were wrong. They all pitched the message to reluctant investors that to be second in online was too late.

However, to be second is, as high tech experience shows, a good place to end up, as long as you have absorbed the mistakes of the people who went first. It does not matter that you are second, what matters is that you are best. Not best in absolute terms but perceived to be best. There is now enough experience in online technology to show two things:

▪ Open is powerful

▪ Second is best.

'Open' is a difficult idea but easy to explain by example. Many new entrants to new technology offer a closed product; Apple offered a computer where it was difficult to write applications because initially the operating system (the guts of the computer) was bundled up in the computer. In the UK, Acorn Computers (who in 1986 had 70% of the UK PC market) made the same mistake.

However, the fickle new consumer dynamited all that. If the consumer wants exactly what they want when they want it this is very hard to satisfy with closed standards. Software simply can't evolve fast enough to meet this kind of demand, if the operating system it has to work on is secret.

It is a nauseating fact in Cupertino, the headquarters of Apple Computers, that Gates got there with what Apple fanatics believe is 'second rate' software. On the shelf of the Quicktime team (who have created a superb series of 3-D software) is a beer bottle with the label 'Microsoft brain wash' on it. However, second is good enough if your software is open and outperforms what went before.

The supply chain of the personal computer industry shows why this is so (Figure 2.5). Anyone seeking to invade the chain might easily expect all the profit to be with the retailers. But this is not so. In fact the profit lies almost entirely at the supply end, in the operating system and the software. That is because Microsoft has managed to use both these

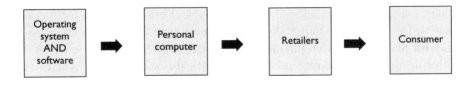

Figure 2.5 Supply chain in the personal computer industry

elements to standardize everything else in the chain. If it doesn't use the Windows operating system it will be impossible to use our software on it, think the buyers.

Microsoft managed to achieve complete domination of its supply chain by being second. It was second into operating systems behind CP/M (who remembers that now?). It was second into most application software, for example Microsoft's word processing application, Word, was based on WordPerfect, which was overambitious and had so many bugs in it that it lost consumer confidence. Microsoft learnt from the pioneers and then added just enough extra benefits to eclipse them.

Its domination is so complete that PC manufacturers have discovered that they are shipping a commodity. PCs are bought almost entirely on price, such margins as they get Microsoft allows them to have. That is why they are called 'fat slaves' because they are entirely dependent for their profits on a master higher up the supply chain.

Many online enterprises are trying to achieve Microsoft nirvana today. The business strategies of many B2B businesses are designed to get high up the supply chain and then standardize it. But it is an expensive strategy, and to achieve it successfully you need a lot of critical mass and a big market presence.

However, by watching what is happening to supply chains, it is often possible to see that a market requires an open standard and then provide it. Coming second is then, by definition, the only way to capture a confused market crying out for standardization.

Attacking the fat

A warning about the fat in an online chain – the party won't last if parts of the chain are spectacularly profitable. This is a normal law of business and there is evidence that it is also becoming true of online.

For example, digital television in the UK (one of the first digital TV systems in the world) has seen most of the early gains go to Murdoch's BSkyB. But such is the margin BSkyB is getting at the end of the supply chain that price cutters have come in to try and grab a section for themselves. For example, Ondigital, a rival, is now offering a year's subscription for just £150 upfront payment (about half BSkyB's rate). It is worth it offering that as the direct relationship with the television consumer is so valuable.

Similarly the BBC could re-enter the battle for viewers if it stopped concentrating on the ratings of its main TV channel and sought to do a deal for heavily discounted access to digital channels and content. By 2010 everyone in the UK will have to receive their television via digital. The cost cutters who can offer quality content could yet win. However, they have to be clever enough to see the opportunity.

CHECKPOINTS

■ Analyse the supply chain of the market you wish to attack.

■ Attack in strength where the margin is highest – well financed and well publicized.

■ See if there is an opportunity to standardize the supply chain around your product as this leads to the highest profits available.

CHAPTER 3

The Technology Test

The simplest mistake you can make in online is to forget to ask the question 'should this business be online at all?' The telephone has been around since Alexander Graham Bell and is a good way of supporting a lot of businesses. Transferring a business to online, whether it be the internet, mobile phones or digital TV, may not reach your target audience and may even be the wrong medium.

Eventually many businesses may use computer-based technology but, for now, in the UK only about a third of the population have internet access. So if you are aiming for a very broad market you will need to plan to reach the other two-thirds in a variety of other ways. The migration of internet services to digital television will broaden this. But start-up online businesses will have to plan to talk to customers using many different electronic channels (including the telephone) before then.

In the US, two-thirds of the population have internet access so the internet is a much more compelling way of reaching many consumers. However, even then it may have its drawbacks.

Keyboards and human intelligence

Eventually the internet, or its successor, will become more intuitive, flexible, faster and much easier to use. The dominant means of online communication remains, at the time of writing, the alphanumeric keyboard, a device which has changed little since it was devised by Remingtons for typewriters at the turn of the last century. Mobile phones have a fiddly, hybrid version which is even worse. Keyboards impede online communication, and the telephone is still ergonomically easier, which is why Microsoft is sinking so much money into voice recognition as a means of controlling PCs and the internet. But for now we are stuck with the alphanumeric keyboard and it puts some people off.

There is also a subtler problem with the internet: it rarely possesses human intelligence. This means that when you talk to it you are usually talking to a computer database, which is programmed to pass on responses that are useful to you. Some online systems are brilliant at this, almost to the point that you think you are dealing with a human being.[1] Sometimes, as with 'instant messenger' (a live e-mail service), you are actually dealing with a human being. The film *You've Got Mail* famously features a moment when both Tom Hanks and Meg Ryan realize that they are logged on simultaneously and can communicate 'as live'. But mainly the internet does not possess human thoughts and sensibilities and this may be a problem for your business.

Take savings and loans. One of the first businesses to be attacked by online invaders was the mortgage (home loan) business. Eloan.com, in the US, did a brilliant job creating an online substitute for the role of the traditional financial adviser. It was set up by two Palo Alto financial advisers, who calculated that selecting a mortgage was straightforward enough for keyboard and internet literate consumers to do by themselves directly, if they were given the data which a US financial adviser has at his or her fingertips.

In the US, mortgages have fixed interest rates and the main difference between loans is the interest rates and charges. However, in places such as the UK, mortgages have variable interest rates and lenders also complicate the products by charging a discounted rate for the first few years, combined with a cornucopia of early redemption fees and cash incentives. European lenders, in short, hold the international award for loan product confusion.

When a few brave online entrepreneurs tried to transfer the US online loan model to the UK, things began to go wrong. Consumers, when asked their views about mortgage websites, said they preferred 'to use an adviser'. They liked to use the sites to find information about loans and compare rates but not to obtain loans directly. This was good for the consumer but bad for the online mortgage businesses, as the businesses planned to make money from commission on completed loans.

Essentially what went wrong is that UK mortgages are too complicated to be dealt with adequately by the present state of computer communication. That is not the same as saying that computers cannot deal with the complexity of UK loans – they can – *but consumers do not trust computers to explain it to them*. They want to perceive a live human intelligence helping them with the transaction. So while telephone mortgage services have done well in the UK, internet-based ones have struggled.

It may be that eventually consumers will trust computer intelligence enough to take them through the complexities of buying a house. But for now investing in software to do this is risky. Better to stick to the telephone.

Using online to drive up costs

This sounds implausible but companies do it. It often happens when a company decides that it must be seen to be online at all costs, usually because it will drive up the share price. However, the way in which the online technology is implemented means that the company cannot possibly be saving money.

It is not worth going online unless you are going to create a significant advantage over your competitors. Companies which drive up costs by going online are normally superserving their customers. However, this advantage is not sustainable unless it produces cost benefits or increases market share. Often it does neither. The solution to this online underperformance is normally a radical change in the way in which that company does business which many traditional companies are simply not prepared to make.

The Aladdin syndrome

An example is the leading UK retailer Tesco. A comparison between Tesco's online model and what has happened in the US illustrates the need for radical thinking in order to get the benefits out of the technology.

Tesco has made much out of its Tesco Online service. It claimed in a November 2000 announcement that it would manage to increase sales due to the rapid expansion of the home-delivery operation and a higher number of stores. 'Some 40 per cent of our internet shoppers were not Tesco customers before', the group said. 'We reckon that with nationwide internet coverage, and more stores, we will probably manage to beat last year.'[2]

Tesco has constructed its online operation on the back of its existing bricks and mortar operation. This means that it uses its existing superstores to receive orders from online shoppers in the locality, which deliver to the customer's home.

But this increases costs. The reason that supermarkets were created was to get shoppers to drive to them and then do the selection, packing and distribution themselves. This significantly lowered the costs of retailing at the time. The effect of employing someone to walk around the store putting orders together and then someone to deliver it to the door are costs that didn't exist before. So the net effect of Tesco's move into online is greater expense.

All home delivery operations face other costs. For example, however the order was taken, a significant number of customers always say that what is sent is wrong. Home delivery services have little choice but to admit culpability, regardless of where the error arose. The only kind of operation which does home delivery well is one where customers are all well known to the distributor and where the extra sales produce marginal cost. It's called a corner store, which the supermarket chains replaced.

It is not clear why Tesco introduced such an overhead except to enhance the share price in a world in which investors were obsessed by the internet. Tesco is saying that 40% of its internet customers were not previously Tesco customers. In effect it is saying that it has increased market share, but at what cost? And will these new customers remain expensive to service?

The truth is that Tesco is caught in the Aladdin syndrome which causes many online ventures in traditional companies to be still born. The Aladdin syndrome says that, in order to progress effectively, you have to give up the old completely for the new ('new lamps for old' as the line in the pantomime goes). However, abandoning old ways of doing things is considered too risky by the boards of most companies so they cling tenaciously to them. But this results in them doing online in a wasteful and expensive way.

Any board facing such a decision should first ask itself whether it is ready or committed to go online, as it must realize that any initiative which increases costs by going online should be classified as an investor relations exercise and not a commercial proposition.

Brain wipes

So how can home delivery be achieved profitably online? The first challenge is to clear your mind completely of preconceptions that you have about how your business should be done. In effect, you have to perform a complete brain wipe of all your assumptions about doing your business. This leads to the first law of online which is:

It is far easier to design a successful online business in a market in which you have *not* been trained than in one about which you have been well taught.

Training is a double-edged sword in that it gives you a set of intellectual tools which are useful but also gives you a set of prejudices which are unhelpful in online creation. This is one area in which consultants can be usefully employed as they need to be set the task of thinking outside your business in order to come up with an online model of how it might work in practice.

It is often best to employ someone from another industry with proven business skills. That is how Daniel Nissan came up with the plan for Netgrocer.com, which is a US-based online grocery seller with a beautiful and cost-effective business model. Nissan's advantage was that he came from the telecommunications industry and had never done a day's work in food retailing in his life.

Nissan analysed the grocery industry as essentially a problem of delivery and not, as supermarkets do, a problem of warehousing. In a supermarket, a lot of resources and time go into creating a customer-friendly, large, appealing 'warehouse' in order to encourage the customer to come to you. However, in the online world, the important element in the supply chain is the immense problem of home delivery as that will give you the edge over traditional retailers.

He set about creating supply deals. The other mental chain which he managed to break is the idea that grocery selling should be local. Enter the Tesco site and it will ask for your postcode, as that determines whether there is a supermarket near enough to deliver to you. But supply deals don't care about distance – get the deal right and you can deliver anywhere at a reasonable price.

That is what Daniel Nissan did. He negotiated a deal with Federal Express to deliver anywhere in the US from their hub at Houston. It was therefore logical to base his warehouse at the airport as it didn't matter where his stock was kept, as long as it was connected to the web and could accept orders. His company headquarters (and his website) he then sited in New Jersey. The company location is almost irrelevant in online, although it helps if stock market analysts can easily make their way to it.

A customer orders via the website (www.netgrocer.com). Their order is sent automatically to the Netgrocer warehouse in Houston where the parcel is packed robotically. The parcels are then despatched from Houston by Federal Express. Much of the US will receive them in four days (the dark shaded area), however, on both coasts there are states where orders are received within two days (Figure 3.1).

What Netgrocer has done is stand the traditional grocery business model on its head by taking full advantage of the cost saving and efficiencies allowed by internet ordering. However, it is not hard to see that someone

Figure 3.1 Areas of the US served by Netgrocer

from a supermarket background would have had difficulty creating this model. Their first question would have been 'where is the supermarket?' to which the answer is 'there aren't any – we don't need them'.

Few online business models so beautifully illustrate that in order to win at online you have to think creatively. That is not the same as saying 'create a model which is wacky and doesn't work', but create something which meets the demands of the new consumer and literally pulls costs out of old business models (while preserving their revenues).

Netgrocer does not need:

- Hundreds of supermarkets serving localities across the country

- Hundreds of car parking spaces for shoppers

- A stock distribution chain to its supermarkets

- People operating cash tills

- People packing food

- Complex management

- Hundreds of people in call centres answering telephones.

The important lesson is that it is an operation which works best and cheapest using the internet. Those are the best reasons for creating an online enterprise.

Stick to online

An important lesson which is emerging from companies which have successfully milked the benefits of the new technology is how easy it is to stray back into the old way of doing things and so lose your edge. This is hardly surprising as the gravitational pull of the old is enormous and the new is often very volatile. It is rather like the mill owners of the Industrial Revolution who, rather than put their surplus capital into more new technology, put it instead into land, agriculture and a country house.

Toys R Amazon

One of the most salutary lessons of recent times is that of Amazon.com when they went into toy retailing in 1999.

Amazon started off with a brilliantly efficient online idea; get consumers to order books online, only keep a small line of stocks, and re-order as soon as the computer technology tells you that you are about to go out of stock. Amazon relied on the ability of computers to keep an accurate track of demand and stocks in order to minimize its borrowing requirements. As Jeff Bezos, Amazon's founder said; 'retailers make the sales forecasts and publishers take the inventory risk'.[3]

But Amazon was seduced by toys. They decided to diversify ahead of Christmas 1999 and toys seemed the obvious choice; they were often small, could be home delivered, were bought as gifts (like a lot of books) and could reasonably be selected from an online catalogue.

However, toys have characteristics which do not fit Amazon's model. Eighty per cent of toy sales are in the two months before Christmas, and toy retailers have to predict what will and what won't sell six months in advance, and then are not allowed to return unsold products. In other words, in the toy market, the *retailer* takes the stock risk, and it is a very hefty risk as it is based on intuition.

Amazon fell into this trap and sold $95 million of toys in 1999 but had to take a $39 million charge to cover the cost of toys it bought but was unable to sell.

However, Amazon's saving grace was (and is) that it is very good at delivery. One of its toy rivals, Toys R Us, had also created an online operation, but while they understood the pitfalls of toy inventory, they were very bad at home delivery. In fact, they were spectacularly bad and were fined $350,000 by the US trade regulator for continuing to make promises they could not deliver.

As a result, Amazon has done a deal with Toys R Us to create a merged online toy service. Toys R Us takes over their toy inventory and Amazon does the deliveries for them.

It is an example of where Amazon, with a superb business model, managed to dilute its competitive edge by assuming a liability which it had managed to evade using online.

So if online has delivered you a competitive advantage (which is the only reason the technology should be used in the first place), don't throw it away in your next move.

CHECKPOINTS

■ You should not go online if the business you are proposing requires direct, simultaneous contact with human intelligence to make a sale (such as the UK mortgage market).

■ You should not go online if you will actually drive up your business costs by using the new technology. You may be tempted to ignore this if going online will drive up your share price but remember that this effect may only be temporary.

■ Be prepared to ditch everything you have ever been taught about how a market you are familiar with should operate. Use consultants to try and think outside your mindset if you find this difficult.

CHAPTER 4

Timing

Two things bedevil online ideas; they can be either ahead of the market or ahead of the technology. Being ahead of either means years of losses before the business comes right, and even when it does come right the debt can drag the business over. Therefore, getting the timing right is not optional – it is essential.

One of the most pernicious myths perpetrated in the great online boom (which ran for roughly nine months until March 2000) is that you have to be first in a market to dominate a market. It is a boom time fallacy. The real truth, the second law of online, is very different:

> To be successful an online business has to be the best in a market which truly exists, at a time when its technology will give it a real competitive advantage.

The principle thing about this truth is that there is no mention of being *first*. It is possible to be first and not to be:

- Best

- In a market which exists

- Using technology which gives you a competitive advantage.

If you have none of these I can confidently predict your business is highly unlikely to make a profit, ever. This is the reason why many of the online pioneers have foundered. They were first when being first to market wasn't (and isn't) the important issue.

The first company to sell clothes by letting buyers see them on the screens in three dimensions, Boo.com, went bust. It was not that it was not first in this market (it was). It was that the technology was not there to support its product. Not enough people had sophisticated enough browsers to allow them the benefit of Boo's three-dimensional viewing.

The same applies to Prestel. Prestel was first into the 'information down a telephone line and onto a PC market'. In fact, it was first by about ten years, as it was launched in the UK in the mid-1980s. Surely it should have taken off like a rocket as it was an early version of the internet?

But Prestel was way ahead of its market. There was an insufficient population of PC users (they were called 'micros' then) to give it critical mass. Very few people understood that you could get anything other than a voice down a telephone line. Surely 'it was like TV – and TV was better?' or so consumers of the mid-1980s thought. More fundamentally, there were simply not enough consumers around with a desperate need for instant information, none of the affluent, time-poor consumers we see everywhere today. They were quite happy with the infrequency of television information and so television stayed king and the micro, and its Prestel card, remained the preserve of hobbyists and travel agents.

So technology timing and market timing do matter a great deal. A very efficient way to lose money is to invest in an online enterprise and then find the technology isn't there to support it.

The technology trap

It is too easy, particularly if you believe in being first to market, to get caught out by the technology trap. Accumulating large debts tends to be an early warning sign that the chief executive is betting heavily on technology (or the market) advancing fast enough to bale out his vision. For example, the telecommunications companies were all betting heavily on third generation mobile telephony in the UK and paid quite staggering amounts for the licences (£27 billion in total). They were betting first that the technology will deliver everything that it promises to deliver, and second that the market will actually want those benefits when they arrive.

When an online entrepreneur is deciding whether or not to raise money to back an idea, they need to be sure that:

- The technology is there to support the proposed system

- The technology, if it is there, is available at a reasonable price.

The second test is almost more important than the first, as the technology is often available but is so pricey that only NASA can afford it.

The object lesson in how to fall head first into the technology trap is the development (or lack of development) of the video on demand industry in the UK.

Video on demand is, on the face of it, a fabulous opportunity. The new consumer doesn't want to be bothered with TV schedules. He or she wants exactly what they want when they want it and can afford to pay for it. So giving the consumer a system where they can watch any programme at the press of a keypad has to be a winner.

Unfortunately, it has been a way to lose a lot of money because the technology to deliver video on demand is expensive to install and expensive to rent.

Three players in the UK know this to their cost: Video Networks, Yes Television and Future TV. Of the three, Future TV has the most radical vision; not only video on demand but also a television service which monitors what the viewer watches and suggests new programmes to him or her which might be of interest. After all, if there are 10,000 programmes on the system all ready to play immediately, the viewer is going to need some help making a selection. Why not have a computer which knows your tastes and does it for you?

All three systems have slightly different business models. For example, Video Networks owns all the components in the chain to the viewer: the programme, the servers and the box which connects to the viewer's television. Yes Television, on the other hand, only supplies content and the means to access it – it relies on other people's networks to create the final link to the viewer.

Indeed the market has taken an eternity to develop because the technology to get video on demand into the home is dependent on the last link of the telephone system into the home, the 'local loop', and this is almost completely controlled by British Telecommunications (BT).

If BT had a record of innovation equivalent to Intel's or General Electric's, this might have been all right. However, BT does not, and can only come up with technology which is so expensive and cumbersome to install that, at the time of writing, they are charging a connection fee of £720 and a monthly rental fee of £52 for video on demand equipment.

To stay in the business, the new video on demand companies have to pay most of this in order to hide the full cost of the service from price sensitive early adopters. So Video Networks has to pay £8 million in fixed costs a year (mainly to BT) just to stay in business.

This produces a technology blockage as the technology necessary for the adoption of video on demand is not available at a reasonable price. So video on demand operators are borrowing in the hope that soon the price will come down and the service will become affordable to the viewer. This makes them vulnerable to established digital television operators, such as BSkyB, coming in with a video on demand on their own established systems when the technology becomes truly affordable. In other words, the core problem of the new video on demand operators is that the technology gives them no real present or future competitive advantage.

It is a similar story with broadband data lines. Yes, they are available, but at a price which makes them unaffordable. This bottleneck is now holding up the development of the internet itself as PCs have more processing and memory than can confer any more useful benefits to the user, unless the user can get a massive increase in data stream off the internet and into the PC. In other words, the broadband blockage may affect PC sales, as consumers ask why they should upgrade when they can see no obvious increase in internet performance.

Therefore, any online proposition must examine whether the technology adopted in the business plan gives enough of a competitive advantage for long enough to establish a firm share of their intended market.

Technological defence

A good example of successful technology timing is the introduction of Sky Active. Sky Digital started its digital TV service in October 1997, offering a greatly enlarged number of conventional channels and pay TV. Pay TV introduced the idea of the viewer paying per programme, allowing viewers instant access to first run movies and sports events. However, none of this was video on demand, pay per view events being started at 30-minute intervals, so viewers had to 'hop onto' the service to see a film ('near video on demand' as it is called).

However, it meant that Sky was able to market products immediately which were supported by the level of available technology, not technology which was promised or expected soon.

Video on demand via the telephone became a serious threat over the course of the year 2000. However, BSkyB knew that it was limited to areas in which telephone exchanges had been upgraded to offer this service and that there was infighting between BT, which owned telephone lines into the home, and the owners of video on demand movie and sports rights who were trying to get rights to use the local loop into the home.

So BSkyB's technology strategy had to be to enhance the existing provisions without getting caught up in the political infighting of delivering video on demand via the telephone line. This would block the line of attack of video on demand services. Again, it was a question of not necessarily being first but of delivering technology at a reasonable price. It achieved this by upgrading some software which was always present in its digital set-top box but which had, until then, only been used to allow viewers access to channels and services to which they were entitled – 'conditional access software'. This software, made by NDS, was also capable of allowing in bits of video on demand in parallel with an existing service, so that, for example, it allowed football viewers to watch a game from any camera at a game. It also allowed news viewers to choose from a series of news items and run them when they chose.

This is not quite video on demand, but is so close that it distracts the viewer from cancelling their BSkyB subscription. It is deliverable now and blocks competitors from creating a technological competitive advantage. In other words, it is a brilliant use of available technology to disarm new technology.

In fact the video on demand services which have launched in Europe have attracted custom through bundling an ISDN line (128kb/sec) with the video on demand service, which significantly undercuts the going rate for ISDN. As with many technologies, video on demand is being bought for something for which it was not intended – also the ultimate fate of Prestel.

Ahead of the market

Entrepreneurs are often right. They work out that one day people will use computers to communicate, but if they are ten years too early (as Prestel was), they will lose money. There was simply no market, in the case of Prestel, to support a very original vision. Yet ten years later that same market was creating a stock market boom. It is no good being right in principle and wrong on timing.

This is the curse of many online enterprises. A great proposition but the market isn't ready for it yet. So often online businesses put in stepping stones, which lead the customer to their vision of the future, but take it in easy stages, using conventional products on the way. This section gives some examples of how to do this.

The essential truth is that it is always better (and safer) to set up in a known online market than an unexplored one. Leave the pioneering to the cash rich and the brave.

And that is the third rule of online markets:

never go into a market with which you are completely unfamiliar.

Surely that rules out a lot of pioneering ventures? The answer is 'yes – it does'. But even with copious market research on a new market, and with prodigious marketing spend, you will never really know if the consumer is ready for your products until you are up and trading.

Into the unknown

With so many online markets completely unexplored, it is very difficult to stay out of unknown territory and so caution is recommended. In fact, the best way to tackle most unknown territory is to get into it via a traditional market.

Baltimore.com has used this method to grow its business. Dublin-based Baltimore is a global company with a huge presence in the US. It sells encryption technology which is the basis of many important services such as payments, transactions and e-procurement. The problem is that initially the market for online security did not exist because potential customers didn't know they needed it. Baltimore has a very large and well-developed consultancy service selling consultancy to clients who think they may have a security problem but are not sure what to do about it.

Baltimore's products are complex and rely on customers recognizing that they will be transmitting confidential information via the internet and that this information needs to be encrypted and decrypted, and signed by the sender to authenticate the information. Such systems are vital in the transmission of payments over the internet, for example.

However, its products involve such abstruse subjects as public key encryption, so, rather than sell public key encryption, Baltimore begins by selling consultancy on encryption and security. In fact only 51% of Baltimore's revenues of £20.1 million in 2000 came from licensing software. The rest was mainly consultancy and profits from subsidiaries.

This approach is clearly only a stepping stone until the day when the majority of Baltimore's revenue will come from licensing. The reason is that by then most customers will understand why encryption and digital signatures are essential to e-business. Also, and more subtly, there should be more competition in the area, which means that customers will be less willing to buy security consultancy which always ends up recommending Baltimore products. Customers by then will not be trying to correct their ignorance but will be well informed enough to shop around.

Showing the benefit

Many online ideas rely on a software product (or products) which, like Baltimore's, are hard to explain in a sentence. This always makes developing a market difficult as it means that the market has to learn before it will buy. Baltimore's solution is consultancy but another more potent one is *benefit*. If you can show the consumer a benefit which comes directly from using the software they won't need to understand it, any more than they need to understand the mechanics of a car in order to see that it is a convenient and fast method of transport.

This often means that useful, ingenious pieces of online software aren't marketed directly but are marketed as something which solves an existing problem. In this way entrepreneurs can synchronize with the current needs of the market and not with a market which they would like to exist.

For example, Philip Gaffrey of Cambridge Advanced Electronics (CAE) has created software which allows users to download very large files in chunks of their own choosing. In other words, if a recipient turns off their computer in the middle of a download, or even switches to another programme, the data is not lost. The download simply recommences, when the computer is switched on again, from the point at which the download stopped. However, this is a hard concept to sell.

So CAE sells the service as a way of transferring large files in the graphics industry. Marketing, advertising and graphics agencies have an insatiable need to transfer large files between themselves and clients, mainly for approvals and sign-offs. The systems available at the moment are expensive to install (notably ISDN lines with 128 kb/sec capacity), so CAE provides a cheap substitute which uses the conventional internet.

This is a way of pump priming the market to make more use of CAE's basic software and encouraging potential users to develop other applications, for example in the video on demand industry. But it provides a way of synchronizing with the present market where there is a need without engaging in the time-consuming business of educating a market through consultancy.

Timing an ambush

It is possible to time the entry of technology into a market so that it completely ambushes the existing players. Here timing and relevant technology have to coincide with a smug, complacent, existing industry. These circumstances are rare but where they exist they make the assailant a lot of money, as the ambushed will bid huge sums of money to try to acquire the attacking technology.

California-based Napster.com hit the worldwide recording industry at just the right moment. The recording industry knew that it was possible to download songs in digital form from the internet but had no strategy for dealing with this threat other than enforcing their copyright to the songs in the courts. This tactic was rather like trying to stop a flood by putting a finger in a leaking dyke. It makes a good story but works badly in reality. The reality the record industry faced was that once the market showed an appetite for downloading songs over the internet it would be difficult to resist the will of the consumer whatever the legal arguments.

When Shawn Fanning started an internet-based service which allowed users to swap music files for free, a showdown was inevitable. Napster. com is in fact the fastest growing internet application ever tracked by research company Jupiter Media Metrix, accumulating 38 million users in its first year.

In reply, the record industry banded together to collectively sue Napster for infringement of copyright. But Napster's timing had been immaculate. It had demonstrated:

▪ Technology which gave it a present competitive advantage (the recording industry had nothing like it)

▪ An existing market – the record industry couldn't argue with 38 million users

▪ It was best – there was no other serious competition in the downloading market.

In retrospect, what the recording industry should have done was to create a market for cheap swappable music files. However, it was that old weakness, they lacked the mindset. They had made a lot of money out of selling music on bits of plastic or vinyl for almost 100 years. Who was this 19-year-old Fanning? Was it likely that he could overturn their business model?

He could. It did not take long before the court action started to crumble because one of the big music industry players, Bertlesmann AG, broke ranks and cut a deal to take a stake in Napster. In the end the market interest and the competitive advantage demonstrated by the technology was just too great. The battle continues with a $1 billion offer in rights payments to the recording industry.

However, the real genius of Napster was timing. It struck at the moment when the market was there, with internet access widespread enough to make the system impossible to ignore. It also had technology which worked and was easy to use. It had little need of expensive publicity as word of the benefit of the system spread spontaneously and worldwide across the internet.

Getting the timing exactly right can make your online business completely unstoppable. However, few online businesses manage to achieve this. If they did, this book would only be as long as this chapter.

CHECKPOINTS

■ To be successful an online business has to be:

  ■ Best

  ■ In a market which exists

  ■ Using technology which gives you a competitive advantage.

■ Before investing in an online idea, check that:

  ■ The market is there for its product

  ■ Affordable technology exists to support that product.

■ Never enter a market with which you are completely unfamiliar

CHAPTER 5

Defining the Market

All online markets are very recent. For example, there may have been stock-broking for many years but there has only been *online* stockbroking for about three. When the online brokers set out, they did not know:

- Whether there was a market for online stockbroking

- How that market would segment

- How they should charge for their services

- What kind of people would use their services.

Most troubling is that no one in an online market knows how fast that market will grow and when it will peak. This is important because it defines whether there is enough of that market for all the businesses in it and whether your business will ever be profitable.

This requires new and disciplined thinking by entrepreneurs. In the past 150 years there have been few opportunities to create entirely new markets, now every existing market structure is being looked at afresh and challenged by online. But it is one thing to think that a market can be rede-fined and quite another to do it in practice. When online companies go wrong it is often because they spot too late that the new market they are leading just hasn't materialized; the consumer simply won't buy in it.

The question is then:

- Does the market exist in any shape or form? If not, it would be better to stop investing in it.

- Have you defined the market correctly?

The market for online brokers, for example, seems to be peaking already. The UK's online investors actually declined by 2% in the third quarter of 2000 and the number of trades executed online was stagnant at 21% of all trades.

So should entrepreneurs abandon the online broking market? The answer is no, they should review:

- The part of it they are in

- What they do in it

- Whether they have the money to redefine what they are doing.

By and large, where there is any demand for online services (and clearly there is for online broking), there is some sector of the market which is growing and profitable. In fact, Germany is extraordinarily promising in online broking, with seven times as many online traders as the UK and 13% growth.[1]

Some careful analysis of emerging online markets repays dividends. It appears that online trading is very sensitive to a bull market in high tech stocks. If high tech stocks fall a lot then trading declines. This is hardly surprising as you would expect online traders to be technologically literate and try to trade high tech stocks for a quick profit. Some things are more difficult to explain, such as why online trading in the UK is so much less popular than it is in Germany. Are brokers' prices higher in Germany? Do investors distrust traditional brokers more in Germany? Someone entering the online broking market needs answers to these questions to see if there is enough demand to allow him or her to make a profit. Later in the chapter there is a method for checking out an online market and whether you have the correct product set for it.

Is there a market?

Defining a market is very important as it allows a company to gain market leadership. For example, Bill Gates was always very clear that he was in the PC software and not the hardware market, because he thought that in the end the hardware would be standardized and people would only pay high prices for the clever bit, the software. He was brave to do this as previously computers had been sold as hardware with essential software bundled up in the hardware sale price. But having defined the PC software market, he proceeded to dominate it.

Market leadership is very powerful as market leaders can:

- Set the pricing and profitability of the market they dominate

- Determine how that market develops (through new products)

- Determine how products are sold (for example, internet access should not be charged for and that revenue should come from other charges).

Market leadership is only exceeded in pure marketing power by standardization, that is, the ability to set the standard for an industry. For example, Microsoft now sets the standard for PC functionality through its operating system. Everyone else in that market, such as applications makers, hardware sellers and peripheral manufacturers, is at the mercy of the standard setter.

The entrepreneurs to be most admired are the ones who enter an online market, experiment with it, decide there is nothing there and exit with their business intact. This will happen a lot in the new economy, and will lead to riches as eventually these operators will know a market so well that they will know when to invest and when to pull out.

There's nothing there

The greatest ability in online is to know when there is nothing there. This is often difficult to do as at that stage a well-funded online operator may have spent millions trying to prove the concept. Then they will have to perform the most difficult contortion in human psychology, which is to say that although you used to think you were right, now you have to admit that you are wrong.

The best exercise is to set benchmarks. If you have not achieved a target on the business plan by a certain date, ask yourself why it wasn't achieved. If you can explain why this is so, correct the mistakes (if you can afford to) and try again.

For example, in November 2000 the UK's first listed dot.com decided to close down. It wasn't insolvent, it just decided that there was no market in what it was doing. Easier.co.uk allowed investors to buy and sell houses for free on the internet. Their business then sold the details of individuals using the service to financial companies. It was a brave attempt to redefine the estate agency market, by making money on the sale of data instead of making money on the sale of property.

However, the financial companies to whom Easier sold data (who were looking to use these lists to expand into operations such as online banking) found that the information did not lead to as many transactions as they had expected. So the business model did not work. But rather than use the remaining £5 million of the £11 million Easier raised at flotation, it decided to sell the business's assets and use the money to move into something more profitable. This is brilliant tactics but very hard psychologically.

It'll be all right (I think)

An uncomfortable position to be in is where you believe that a market is there but it is taking so long to emerge that you are haemorrhaging cash in the process. In fact, this means that at best you are ahead of the market (see Chapter 3) and at worst the market isn't there. If you can find more funding to continue you might be able to prove this. If not, you will run out of cash and close. It is the situation in which online entrepreneurs find themselves saying to their backers 'It'll be all right', while hoping they *are* right.

The only way to monitor whether your vision of a new market is correct or incorrect is to set yourself stringent benchmarks *before* you start trading. It is no good afterwards because by then you will have been infected by your own publicity. Everyone is susceptible to their own publicity, it is a psychological fact of life. The trick is not to become a victim of it, which is what happens in too many online failures.

A useful example of this psychology in action is the attempt to develop an online mortgage broking market. Essentially this works on the assumption that people, if given full enough information about a wide variety of mortgages, will be happy to make their own choice and buy mortgages via their personal computer over the internet.

It seems a reasonable proposition that eventually the online consumer will demand exactly the mortgage they want when they want it, and an online service should be the way to deliver that.

Figure 5.1 shows a comparison between the marketing spend and the online applications received by one vigorous entrant into this market. It looks convincing enough; spend on marketing is supporting a rising trend of mortgage applications. This graph was used in a presentation to potential investors in this company. However, it is pure spin and cloaks a depressing truth.

First, the scale on the y axis of the graph is logarithmic, and hides the fact that compared to the spend in pounds the number of mortgage applications is in fact low. By the end of the seven-month period, over which a total of £3.75 million has been spent on marketing, a grand total of 3165 online mortgage applications have been made. Put another way, it has cost

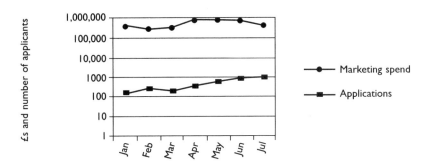

Figure 5.1 Marketing spend against online applications for mortgages

the company over £1000 to deliver each mortgage application. A more accurate portrait of the relationship between marketing spend and applications is shown in Figure 5.2 where the scale is normal.

This shows a sharp decline in marketing spending and also that all the marketing spend has had absolutely no effect in delivering an online mortgage market, in reality the applications are so small as to be insignificant.

There is also one remaining fact which both of these graphs overlook. Of the 3165 applications received, only 87 proceeded all the way through to taking out a mortgage – a conversion rate of 2.75%. However, when the graph (Figure 5.1) was presented to the company, they believed that they were on a rising trend and could get the cost of acquiring new applicants down.

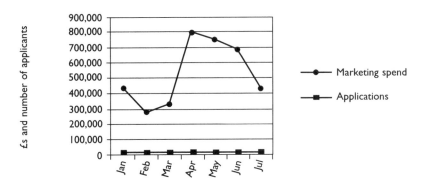

Figure 5.2 Same information using a normal scale

However, one thing stands out starkly from these figures: *this business doesn't work*. The consumer apparently doesn't want to buy their mortgages directly online.

Meanwhile, this business carried on trading for a few months before the inevitable happened and it ran out of cash. The mistake they had made was to believe that their model worked and also that the data they were getting proved it. In reality, the data was presented in a way which fooled even the management. They would have been able to make a far better decision had they set some *simple* performance benchmarks before they started trading and stuck to them.

These benchmarks could have been:

■ The marketing spend in a month /the number of mortgages progressed to completion in that month

■ The marketing spend in a month/the number of hits on the mortgage website that month.

This second benchmark would have shown that awareness of the site was being bought at a cost 50 times that of other online services, in other words it was hard to make consumers use the website at any cost. On seeing these measurements, they should, like Easier.co.uk, have made a fundamental reappraisal of their online plans.

They also made a far more fundamental mistake; they didn't test their products against their target market before they started trading. You cannot define an online market unless you check whether there is a demand somewhere for your proposed products. Nevertheless, it was a brave (if expensive) attempt to define a new market.

Define and lead

Most online start-ups begin by confusing two ideas:

■ What they think is good for a market

■ What that market really wants.

If allowed to persist, this gets online companies into deep trouble as all the development spending will be on software which is appropriate for the market they imagine exists, rather than the one which is really there. When they finally discover that the consumer doesn't want to buy in the way in

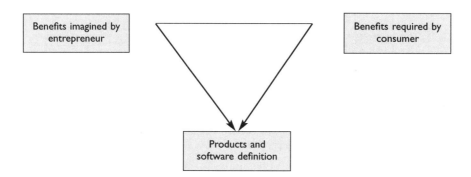

Figure 5.3 Aligning the imagined and real benefits of a product

which the online entrepreneurs expect them to buy, there is an enormous cost in changing their business plan and their technology. By then it is normally too late and the company has run out of cash.

To avoid this some early discipline is needed. The basic process can be summarized by the development triangle (Figure 5.3), where the original benefits which the entrepreneur imagines to flow from his or her company and the benefits actually required by the consumer are made to coincide (through a process which leads to the bottom of the triangle) which gives a blueprint for the products and the software needed to support it.

The fundamental error committed by the online mortgage company was that they had imagined the new consumer wanted a particular service, when in fact the consumer seemed happy enough with the existing service.

These mistakes are best avoided by starting out on the right track. As this problem is common to most online start-ups, a method is available to make online entrepreneurs think about their business, their products and their market before they start spending money on software and marketing.

It is called the 'e-comm market benefit process' (Figure 5.4), and is, in truth, very simple. But its virtue is that it forces online companies to think carefully about what market they are in before they spend investors' money tackling it. It is inexpensive to use and does not require expensive market research to complete it. Three elements need defining:

A Who your customers are (in other words, the target market).

B The benefits which your company will bring to its customers and whether those are the benefits your customers want.

C The products which your customers want in order to receive those benefits.

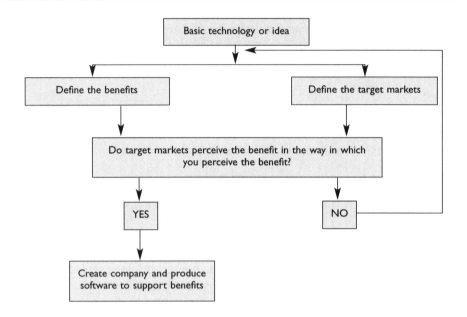

Figure 5.4 e-comm market benefit process

Companies normally get B wrong first time, which is why the process forces you first of all to draw up two lists (benefits and target markets) and then asks you to investigate whether those target markets want those benefits. This results in a simple list of benefits which you know your target customers actually need.

How is this done? The best method seems to be to get the CEO to actually go out and talk to groups of target customers. There is no substitute for this because any focus group research is subject to interpretation and if the CEO actually hears the evidence first hand he or she will tend to believe it more. It is best to go to representatives of your target customers with a proposition and see how they react to both the proposed products and their pricing. Always include pricing because it tests whether customers will actually buy. If they grimace you know that the product might be fine but not at that price level.

If customers reject your proposition, or are politely non-committal, *go back to the drawing board*. At this stage it is merely your time and not someone else's money. You now need to come up with a new product set which does appeal to some of your target customers. The process continues until you have refined it to the stage where you know that once you launch the company there is a market interested in that product.

After that it is simple. Proceed to the last box on the flow chart and commission the software which supports your products. Always produce as detailed a specification as possible, as most software delays are caused by specification changes.

DomainAudit.com – the e-comm market benefit process in action

DomainAudit.com was born out of an idea by Tom Ball, who, like many online entrepreneurs, is still in his twenties. He had realized, back in 1999, that it was possible to create a software system which interrogated all the official databases holding details of domains, thus enabling the automatic registration of a domain anywhere in the world. Using the same technology it was also possible to see who held current domain addresses and how long it was until they expired.

So the impetus for DomainAudit was the technology that made it possible to carry out a particular process for the first time. The first exercise, therefore, was to identify the target customers of such a system. Tom's original idea had been to launch it as a business to consumer service. However, this was a crowded market, with US giants such as Register.com already in it. Also, it seemed that the ability to search and register domain names simultaneously worldwide was of no benefit to the ordinary consumer – who was clearly quite happy with the service he or she was getting from the existing domain registries – in other words, it required a more specialist application.

So it was decided to target businesses. But which businesses needed fast domain name registration? This required some market research into businesses dealing with company registration in general, such as lawyers and accountants.

List A (who the customers are) began to look like this:

- Lawyers

- Accountants

- Legal departments of large companies

- Brokers who registered trademarks

- Consultants

- Venture capitalists.

In fact, in doing this, a large category of potential users were omitted which the company only became aware of when they started trading.

List B (the benefits these customers wanted) took a little time to prepare and involved visiting the staff of law firms, accountants and companies which dealt in company registration. The lawyers did indeed want the ability to search rapidly to see if domain names were available and then register them. However, they also wanted something that hadn't been thought of – a printout of those domains which were free, which were taken, and what conditions and permissions were needed in order to make an effective registration in any country or jurisdiction.

These lawyers made it clear that as long as this printout was well presented and accurate they could charge a very reasonable sum for it, equivalent, in fact, to the sum they could charge for a search for trademarks. In fact, DomainAudit appeared to have stumbled into a sort of electronic trademark market, dealing with the processing, reporting and registration of trademarks for the internet (in other words, domain names).

Companies also had a specialized demand. Departments within corporations had amassed so many domain names over the last three years that they had lost track of what they did and didn't own and when they needed renewing. Therefore, what companies wanted was domain name management, and their need was urgent.

As a result, list B was very different from Tom's original list, which would have looked a bit like this:

- Registration of domain names in any territory for anyone who wants it fast

- Checking on who owns domain names in any territory worldwide.

List B, after the research, had now changed to:

- The ability to check fast and accurately which domains are taken in any territory worldwide

- The ability to produce a printout of domains showing a client what is taken, what could be taken, the cost and the conditions of registration

- The ability to register any domain name anywhere in the world

- The management of domain names – present, past and future.

This was a far more sophisticated list of benefits than would have appeared had DomainAudit gone forward with Tom's original vision.

Clearly this fundamentally affected the product range which had to be produced. Also it affected the way in which the business was positioned, it was now essentially a service supported by software and not simply a piece of software in its own right.

List C was therefore radically different from when the product was first conceived. It now consisted of three core products:

- A worldwide domain search and registration service

- A printout which could be originated from the PC of those using the service, which could then be charged on to clients

- A domain management service looking after domains which companies already own and tracking those which they don't but would like to acquire.

This involved a fundamental rewrite of the software which had been developed up to that point and a delay in launch until it was delivered. Nevertheless, on launch the service was greeted with great interest and one of the first companies to sign up for it was the major UK retailer Marks & Spencer.

However, just because you have launched doesn't mean you should stop testing your company against your market or potential markets. In fact, DomainAudit, on analysis, was first into the international domain management market it had stumbled across and can make a fair claim therefore to market leadership, a point brought out strongly in its launch advertising (Figure 5.5).

After launch, a large new base of potential clients was found in the data management industry. It became apparent that many companies trust domain registration and domain management to their data management suppliers. These companies typically did not feel that they had the expertise to engage in domain management and so were already looking for a subcontractor to carry out this function. This created another lucrative market for DomainAudit, in which it is already market leader.

If your clients are online, you need to call the DA.

Lawyers. Accountants. Bankers. Your clients use independent professionals to manage all of their key assets. Except one: their domain names. Remarkable when you consider that domain names require constant protection, maintenance and monitoring. DomainAudit looks after this whole process. We help you to extend your services into the online arena. We'll handle every aspect of your clients' domain name asset management with maximum confidentiality. Quickly, securely, comprehensively. We're far more than an online resource. We're the first domain name asset management company.

Contact us now. **www.domainaudit.com**

DomainAudit®
Domain Asset Management Services

www.domainaudit.com
34 Park Street, London W1K 2JD

Figure 5.5 DomainAudit launch advertising

CHECKPOINTS

■ Before you launch an online business check:

  ■ Whether your target market exists

  ■ Whether you are approaching it in a way which will allow you to make a profit in it.

■ The most powerful position in any market is that of market leadership. This means that you have defined your market in such a way that you are the biggest player in it. As online is new always try to define a new market in which you will be market leader.

■ There is one position which is even more powerful than market leadership and that is to set and own the standard for a market. However, this is difficult to achieve and hold on to.

■ Always check whether your company is succeeding in a market using clear benchmarks.

  ■ Measure these benchmarks using stark, clear sets of figures. Do not produce figures in order to please an audience – they will mislead your management.

■ Do not be ashamed of admitting you were wrong about a market. It is better to close a business which is not performing than to persist with it.

■ Check whether the benefits which your company will bring to its customers are actually the benefits those customers want.

■ Use the market benefit process analysis to check this.

  ■ You needn't use expensive focus groups – far better if the CEO visits your intended customers and finds out from them what they want and how much they are prepared to pay for it.

CHAPTER 6

Online Branding

Branding remains the only way to give your company an enduring competitive edge in a market.

Businesses (particularly start-ups) often forget what has given names such as Mars, Persil, Disney and Coca-Cola their seeming immortality; these names have all acquired a personality. Nor has this happened by accident, their owners have invested heavily in creating, promoting and reinforcing that personality to their customers. The result is a brand, a number of emotional reasons why people stick with a washing powder or even a mobile phone service.

Branding is the most potent form of marketing and also the most difficult to achieve as it exploits the mysterious depths and undercurrents of human psychology. Many chief executives find this as baffling as the debate over the euro. Greg Dyke, now Director General of the BBC, once rounded in a public debate on the man who had created the Channel 5 brand for him and said 'all branding is bullshit, isn't it?'

However, whether you choose to believe in branding or not, companies which have failed to invest in their branding often succumb to mysterious and sudden corporate illnesses. Ask why Marks & Spencer started losing customers seemingly overnight and no one is quite sure. But Marks & Spencer used to boast about how little they spent on marketing and branding. They felt that getting their goods out onto their counters was enough, but clearly it wasn't.

There are branding gurus who argue that Microsoft would not now be facing dismemberment by the US regulators had it concentrated on investing in its brand rather than boasting about its size and ubiquity.

I believe that branding is about to be changed forever by online technology. That is because many of the things which branding has done for established names for the last 50 years can be done much more effectively using computers. A brand can be made not only to have a personality but also can be made to seem to behave like a person. Traditional branding tries to breathe personality into soap powders, shampoo and chocolate but relies heavily on your personal experience of that product being the same as the public experience which marketers send *at a different time* through media such as television and posters. In online branding the personal experience and the public messages can be simultaneous rather as they are when you check into a good hotel or a fabulous restaurant. This will result in branding becoming one of the critical battlegrounds of the online revolution and one on which market share is held or lost. There are convincing signs that this process has already begun.

Emotional reasoning

Branding is particularly important in online business as it gives customers a series of emotional reasons to stick with you rather than flick to the website down the road. In an area such as online, where it is very easy for someone to imitate your business plan, you need hooks to get people to return to you. And if your business plan is successful, someone will imitate it, that is guaranteed.

So branding, for online businesses, is well worth the investment. In a way branding is like love, it is a reason people return to something, although they find it hard to give the reason they keep going back.

Working out what your brand is and why people will want to love it is a very tricky business. Best to use someone with a track record. Branding experts are a breed apart, combining the skills of a Freudian psychiatrist with the gut instincts of a snake medicine salesman. They are not made, they are born.

Doug Richardson is one such. He did a lot of the thinking behind brands such as the BBC and the Yorkie bar. He sits in an office crowded with piles of paper leaving just enough space on his desk for a cup of coffee and a packet of cigarettes.He spends most of his time staring out of the window, smoking. He is full of strange juxtapositions such as the connection between Brooke Bond tea, Croydon and the film Alien. These are designed to illustrate the feel or essence of a brand both what is right for it, and what is wrong with it. He searches for the emotional hook, the reason people do or do not want to believe in a commercial proposition.

The Yorkie bar was a case in point. Rowntree were looking for a way of taking market share off their rivals Cadbury, at that time producers of the most successful chocolate bar on the UK market. Cadbury's emphasized, rather scientifically, their bar's creaminess. They showed two jugs of milk being poured at the moment of creation of a Cadbury's chocolate bar. Doug could not understand why this campaign was successful. His experience told him people weren't really interested in quantitative science, in much the same way that normal consumers don't care about the speed of an Intel processor.

Then he employed a psychologist to investigate chocolate. The psychologist came to a devastating conclusion. Chocolate was an emotionally charged product, it reminded people of sucking at their mother's breast. Mother's breasts were, among other things, full of creamy, nourishing milk. Remind people about creamy milk in association with chocolate and it reinforced their happy memories of infancy.

Doug, realizing that chocolate bars were about emotion (like all other great brands), came up with a series of emotional attributes for a new chocolate bar from Rowntree – it should be friendly, appealing, the sort of thing you would want to share with people. And so the essential positioning for the Yorkie bar was created, for while Rowntree couldn't beat Cadbury on utility, they could beat them on brand if they could get a different emotional positioning.

All this may seem very distant from online business. But there is a very important point to this story which goes for any type of brand:

▪ consumers are attached to brands primarily for *emotional* reasons and not for reasons of utility.

This is often a lesson which is forgotten by online start-ups, which are frequently the creation of engineers who get their biggest buzz out of clever and innovative software. So, when describing why people will buy their product, they often start by saying 'because it is the most cutting edge ...' and then describe the engineering advance this represents.

Brand stands

People often confuse branding (the process of attaching a series of emotional values to a product) with naming a product. True brands are often embodied in a name but the name is simply part of the whole package of associations with which the marketer is trying to endow it. However, brand names are powerful and are used to endorse or reinforce the pull of a product.

There are three ways in which brand names are used to enhance a product. These are:

1   *Brand naming.* The brand is separate from the product but is used in association with it, to reinforce that the product contains all the values that the main brand embodies, even though that product has an identity of its own. The best example of this is the Ford Motor Company which uses its powerful main brand to enhance its individual products. So consumers can buy a Ford Focus or a Ford Taurus, the main brand and the individual product containing a shared series of values.

2   *Brand and descriptor.* This is where the individual product has no values of its own other than those conferred on it by the main brand. So the product itself is characterized by a description to which is attached the main brand, for example 'Heinz Baked Beans' or 'Heinz Tomato Soup'.

3   *Endorsement.* This is where a powerful brand is kept distant from a product, but is used to endorse it, for example 'Egg from Prudential'.

The lesson for online companies is that you have to decide if you are creating an 'umbrella brand', which is separate from your product. If you are creating more than one product, an umbrella brand is almost essential. Then you have to decide if you want the brand or the products to be the most powerful. Endorsement is only useful to a start-up if you already have a strong brand, but it doesn't have powerful enough connotations to be in the product name. If it does, see if you want your products to have less of an individual profile (descriptor) or a more powerful presence in their own right (naming).

People rarely buy anything because it is a great engineering advance. People buy because your product has got under their emotional skin in some way. Their emotional reasoning should be supported by benefits, some of which may be technological. But at the end of the day these arguments are little understood by buyers and are often spurious. Soap powder makers used to argue that their powder now washed whiter because it was 'blue'. Think about it. Since when did blue equal white? However, it did play to an emotion that the clothes would be shockingly clean, in an age when shocking cleanliness counted. Our present age, more concerned with the environment, has a different series of emotional hot spots.

The second lesson in branding is to remember that:

▪ you are not necessarily the target audience.

The most common fault I come across in online marketing is that start-ups have created emotional reasons which their colleagues would admire and not those of their target market.

DomainAudit is a web start-up which searches for and registers company domain names on behalf of companies which require highly confidential and comprehensive searches. One of the main values they wanted to associate with the product was that it was cutting edge. However their main audience was company secretaries and lawyers. For that audience, which craves confidentiality and security, cutting edge is at worst frightening and at best irrelevant.

DomainAudit, in order to succeed, needed a personality which embodied staid values such as 'established, trusted, secure, confidential'. It resulted in a logo and feel which the creators of DomainAudit would not want for their own company, CD9, one of the UK's most innovative software outfits. But that is not the point. The new brand was designed to appeal to a group of people who are indifferent to software, a market which simply wants a service it can *trust*.

When branding, it is best to think of your product as if it was a service and the online element in it was a tool, which didn't rely on computers at all. What values and personality would you give it to appeal to its intended market? In that way, any engineering marvels it contains will become obscure and irrelevant, as they are to most people who will purchase the system.

America Online (AOL) ran an interesting campaign promoting itself as an internet service provider (ISP). AOL may be big but ISPs are two a penny, so a strong brand is essential to make it stand out from the competition. They created a person called 'Connie' who came out of the computer and told bemused Mums and Dads why the internet was educational and safe for their children (including mention of all kinds of filtering systems which AOL uses so that children can't access unsuitable material).

The point about this campaign, however, was not the filtering systems, or what AOL charged for internet access. It positioned AOL as an educator and guardian of children. Connie herself is like a school teacher, serious, concerned for the kids and very plain. This campaign was about personality and branding, it gave many emotional reasons why your children need AOL if you care about them. A very similar positioning, in fact, to some soap powders.

Case study: the branding of Egg

Egg is the name that was eventually given to the online banking service created by British insurance giant, the Prudential. The Prudential is a highly conservative company (almost to the point of dullness), so when the Prudential went to top UK advertising agency HHCL saying they wanted to create a radical new internet bank, both agreed that the new brand would have to be very eye catching.

The Prudential had analysed the financial market and noticed a move away from the 'hand-holding culture' where a financial adviser guides bemused and confused consumers through the financial jungle (and takes a commission on whatever they are sold). The Prudential had noticed that there was a new generation of consumers coming into the market who were not only confident about manipulating and under-standing financial data but also could gain access to these data via all kinds of electronic channels. (This is interesting as it reinforces this book's argument that the growth of online is primarily a social and not a technological phenomenon.)

However, these were not the type of people who would be attracted to the Prudential, with its paternalistic, hand-holding image.

The Prudential was testing various names for its new banking service and among the front runners were:

- Oxygen
- Egg
- Mint

Mint was playing well as it had the suggestion of 'fresh' and of a coin mint. However Egg won the day, for reasons to do with the way in which HHCL wanted to position the new brand.

HHCL is an unusual advertising agency and is normally chosen because of its radical credentials. In fact, HHCL has branded itself as 'professional radicals' and promotes this as its main selling point, so the Prudential knew that whatever HHCL came up with would certainly be different. HHCL does indeed work in an unusual way. Most adver-tising agencies, when creating a new brand, start with the consumer as their point of reference (Figure 6.1). After all that is what gets drummed into most professionals on marketing courses. Brand creation is traditionally done by interrogating the consumer, working their reactions into a creative proposition, comparing it to the competition and then selling it to the client and their culture.

However, HHCL works by reversing this flow (Figure 6.2). Its argument is that to be truly innovative you can't rely on the consumer, who is heavily influenced by what has gone before. You have to start with the new culture and identity which the client is trying to achieve. So start with the vision of the new business, modify that by compar-ison with what the competition is doing and then turn it into a creative proposition. Finally test this creative proposition with the consumer and see if it flies.

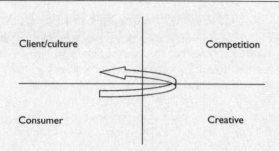

Figure 6.1 Normal method of brand creation and definition

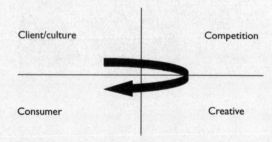

Figure 6.2 HHCL method of brand creation and definition

HHCL worked closely with Mike Harries, the chief executive of Egg, who described his business proposition in a few clear ideas. These were:

- No one can be defined as part of a group or grouping – you are an individual
- Everything should be done for you as an individual
- This is banking just and only for you.

On testing this proposition against the rest of the banking competition, HHCL found that people did not trust existing banks, nor did they understand the language which big banks used. These ideas became an important element in their thinking as they evolved the branding of Egg.

Egg was adopted as the name of the new service as it was warm, positive and an idea which people trust. Being against eggs is rather like being against motherhood, after all.

So HHCL arrived at two essential values for the Egg brand:

- For you and only for you
- Trustworthy, plain talking.

However, Ian Priest, who headed up the HHCL Egg team, was very aware that the big danger in launching a new banking brand, let alone an internet one, is that it has no credibility. And in banking if you don't have credibility, you don't attract customers.

So the Prudential brand (which is an insurance brand) was used as an 'umbrella' brand to endorse the new service. Initially the Egg logo was always accompanied by the words 'from Prudential'.

The advertising campaign went all out for the essential values of Egg. It used well-known young personalities undergoing a lie detector test. They were asked about themselves by a nasty inquisitor and eventually even whether they were being paid for making this advertisement (to which their answer was 'Yes'). The advertising played heavily on the values of plain talking and the untrustworthiness of the competition. This in itself was done in such an unusual way as to make the viewers realize that this was new and different and not a standard banking advertisement.

The radio campaign featured a number of staff from the telephone service dealing with real live customers. This again enhanced the values of 'straight talking' and for you as an individual – and not for stereotypes.

In the end, the launch of Egg was too successful as the service reached its year one subscriber target in a couple of months and the system could not scale up fast enough to cope with the level of demand. Some argue that this was because Egg trumped all existing interest rates on a current account. However, the take-up also shows that Ian Priest's worries about credibility and plain talking had been met through the branding. Before the campaign, Prudential was not a bank and had it set itself up as one (as, say, the 'Prudential Bank') it is unlikely that it would have created the stir, excitement or the customer numbers that its oddly named subsidiary has done.

Online advances into branding

Branding is about giving a product a personality for a very good reason, and that is that personality makes a product 'sticky'. 'Stickiness' is the marketing industry's blunt description of 'a reason to return', what could be described as 'love', if the product was a person and not a thing. However, it's a good concept as extremely successful branding makes a product so sticky that it takes a huge push to dislodge people, even after the benefits of that product have largely disappeared.

Online is exciting because it can create a sticky personality using computer technology. Computers can be used to ape or imitate human characteristics and can give the user the impression that he or she is being remembered and dealt with personally, in the same way a good butler or a five-star hotel would treat you.

What is the essence of a five-star hotel? It knows, quite simply, exactly what you want in the way in which you want it. When you arrive it knows what kind of room you like, how you like your coffee and what paper you want in the morning. It doesn't have to ask – it just knows you so well. Five-star hotels take care to memorize the details of their best customers in this way for a simple reason; it produces repeat business. The hotel knows that you will come back and spend even more money. The hotel knows that knowing you produces the essence of all great brands – stickiness.

Online services can do all this. However, it is amazing how few corporate websites use these techniques. It is as if they consider that a web presence is impassive, like a large hoarding or billboard on the information super-highway which you see briefly as you go by but which is otherwise completely unmemorable. But computers are far cleverer than a hoarding.

Take a very simple device which all browsers can use. The browser is the piece of software which lets users see objects (such as pictures, text or animations) on the internet. Browsers are all fitted with the ability to issue 'cookies'. Cookies are like calling cards and when you go to certain sites they issue your computer with a file, which contains details of who you are and where you have been on that site. This information is kept on your own computer and is called a 'cookie'. Go to 'Start' (if you have a PC), select 'Find' and type in 'cookies' and it will select the folder where your cookies are kept. Open one of them (using an application such as 'wordpad'). It will simply contain a string of a few letters and several numbers, which will be unintelligible unless it is the kind of computer on which websites live – which is called a server.

When an internet user returns to a website which has issued it with a cookie, the server which supports that website can do several things:

- It can identify from the cookie which pages and objects you have visited on its website

- It can often tell your likes and dislikes from preferences you have exhibited when visiting that site before

- It can show you things which it thinks will appeal to you, such as advertisements or bits of information.

Cookies link up with a database which servers hold containing any details that you have given them, for example Amazon.com's database contains details of anything you have bought on the site. Links between a database and a cookie are potentially extremely powerful. On returning to Amazon, users are offered new titles which the software guesses, from looking at your buying patterns, may appeal to you.

This is very powerful branding and is relatively cheap. Online entrepreneurs don't have to charge the rates which five-star hotels do for staff with elephantine memories or filing systems. It is as if when you were entering a supermarket you were stopped at the door by a person who told you where anything that was likely to be of use or interest to you was located. It creates the perception of a service which knows you and cares about you. It creates stickiness as thick as glue.

Cookies are also subtle. It is entirely possible to construct a web page which is different for every user who enters the site, based on the data held on them in the site's database. As soon as their cookie identifies them, the site can offer a doctor the latest medical news, a judge the latest legal news and a journalist the latest on the media. Exactly what they want in the way in which they want it.

This is the essence of stickiness, which is that to believe in a brand a user has to believe that it cares about them. Although this is incredibly expensive to achieve through impersonal advertising (such as television), it is very easy and inexpensive to achieve using web technology.

Case study: the US battle for consumer data

In Europe, consumers have barely woken up to privacy control and protection. However, in the USA there is a small but growing industry which offers consumers ways of selecting the companies to which they give personal data. This recognises the value of individual data in the new economy in general. It may be that as consumers become more web literate a battle will break out between individuals and data accumulators.

For example, Lumeria, based in Berkley California, offers users the opportunity to route their internet access via the Lumeria servers and so stop any personal details being transmitted directly to internet advertisers. This service also allows users to specify the kind of web advertising in which they are interested and so allows only adverts in which the consumer is interested to appear on their PC screen.

iPrivacy of New York is strictly for the paranoid. In iPrivacy's service a user downloads his protection software from a company he knows and trusts, such as his credit card company. The software is capable of cloaking his or her identity. When a user wishes to buy something the programme issues them with a new, fictitious identity and credit card details. The credit card company then honours the payment and sends out the real address details to the e-commerce vendor but with a fictitious name. Fictitious identities are generated only once, making it impossible for e-commerce operators to build up useful or meaningful databases.

At the moment, this sort of sophisticated service is really just for those who are very smart or paranoid (or both). However, there are signs of increasing consumer awareness of the issues in the US. Doubleclick, an online advertising agency based in New York, recently aborted plans to merge its records of people's visits to websites with its database of users names and addresses. This would have allowed advertisers to mailshot people who casually looked at web advertisements. Another company, Toysmart, became the target of press vilification when, to stave off bankruptcy, it tried to sell its customer database to another retailer.

Simultaneity

Cookies create the impression that a product exists entirely for an individual. This contrast with traditional advertising which suggests that products exist for large sections of the public. In a way online could abolish the need for these public messages, as the message which you receive via an online product's website could always be personal. So the promise of the service for you (and only for you) becomes the public message. The implication of this is something which advertisers have yet to absorb fully.

The other essential element to a great brand experience is that the emotional message associated with the brand's advertising is experienced at the same time as the brand is consumed. This is extremely difficult to do and relies heavily on the psychological message being remembered at the time of consumption.

However, online brands are in a position to do this as they can link their brand message with the consumption of the service. Attempts to do this so far have been crude but this is an important area of online stickiness which repays careful thought, as it will, I believe, cause some fundamental debate about the nature of online branding.

Take the word 'new'. Maurice Saatchi claims it is the most powerful word in advertising. Car manufacturers claim their product is 'new' since they know the power of the word, although all they have done to the product is add a new spoiler. However, on online, the message 'new' and the experience of that product can be the same. This is because it is possible to place a small piece of software on your computer which searches for new upgrades to a product every time you go on the web. For example if Hewlett Packard computers produce any new upgrades for their machines a piece of software will detect and download it while you are online.

RealNetworks, the media software company, will tell you via e-mail when to upgrade to a new media player and will provide you with a link to it. It is not merely that the product claims to be new, it is always renewing itself in front of your eyes.

Behaving like the message simultaneously is a forceful area of brand reinforcement. BBC News Online provides an online news ticker. You download it and every time you go online it runs into the corner of your screen and is completely up to date. So BBC News Online not only claims to provide the news but *is* the news every time you go online. Its message is simultaneously reinforced.

Online can do this because the software involved in browser technology supports it. JavaScript, for example, provides a live link between a site's database and a computer user. Three years ago this was not possible, pages only refreshed when the refresh button was pushed. However, now JavaScript provides live links which allow information, pages, charts and pictures to be updated continuously, giving the perception of an experience which is not only personal but spontaneous and up to date. This is delivering everything which TV advertising, which is a series of pre-recorded mass messages, fails to deliver.

Online branding is in its infancy but is a new and formidable field which promises to have a huge impact on traditional forms of advertising and brand thinking. It has already begun to impact on that heavyweight electronic messenger, television.

Television gets personal

Television, since its introduction 50 years ago, has always been an impersonal medium. Broadcasting is an Orwellian business of trying to get as many people as possible to watch and listen simultaneously to the same message. But as Marks & Spencer can tell you, persuading a large number of people to purchase the same thing at the same time is increasingly difficult. It defies the spirit of the times.

Television will have to adapt. It is being gradually forced by many radical technological changes. Indeed, these technological changes will transform the way in which the last century's most powerful advertising medium will market and brand products.

In the next six months, television will be getting much closer to the individual viewer and their tastes. SkyDigital (the digital television market leader in the UK) and TPS (the French equivalent) both offer channels which allow viewers to see a film at certain fixed points. They also offer interactive services where information can be pulled off the screen as the viewer demands it in colourful graphics, pictures and text. TPS's most popular interactive offering is its Meteo weather service where viewers can get three-day forecasts for the area within 20 kilometres of them, all via the TV in their living room.

But this is only the beginning. Digital television takes digital signals and decodes them through a box. This box is, as near as makes no difference, a computer. However, to keep the costs of this computer down it has been stripped of memory, which means that its ability to store and manipulate information has been strictly limited until now.

Sometime in 2001, SkyDigital's set-top boxes with a hard disc will become available in Britain. Figure 6.3 shows a pre-production model. This means that, for the first time, domestic television can behave like a computer. While watching a programme, the set-top box will be able to select and record onto its hard disc any other programme currently available which the viewer indicated an interest in. The box is capable of storing up to 40 hours of programming at a time.

This has huge implications for advertising. For example, if the viewer told the box that he or she wanted to record any home improvement show,

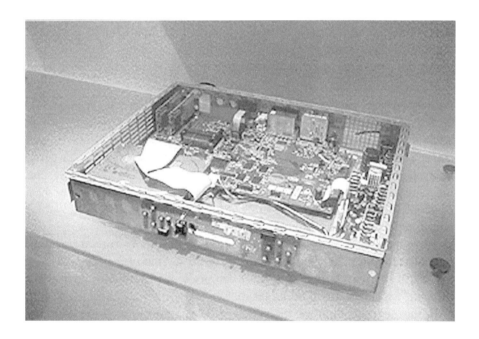

Figure 6.3 Pre-production model of a digital television set-top box capable of storing 40 hours of programming

this would be useful information for advertisers who would then target home improvement products at the viewer. The information held on the viewer by the platform provider (in this case SkyDigital) is also very useful as the viewer's postcode would allow advertisers to send certain advertisements to the hard disc for storage and offer them for viewing when it thinks he or she would be most receptive to them.

In other words, even television is fast becoming a medium in which content and messages are personal to the viewer. The method for sending particular subscribers certain adverts has not yet been worked out and doubtless the UK's luddite television regulators will want to exert some influence over this. However, 'broadcasting' is breaking down and will, I believe, form only a fraction of the way in which people will consume video and information services in the future.

I believe that this process is unstoppable because in reality viewers demand to see very few events at the same time, with the exception, possibly, of some sporting fixtures and important news events. The new consumer will want to see television and advertising at the times they (and only they) want to see it. They will not want to be dictated to by a channel scheduler.

This does cause problems for advertisers, as 80% of a typical campaign is spent on advertising in commercial breaks in traditional channels. If people aren't going to watch traditional channels, how will it be possible to create brand awareness and stickiness among large groups of people? Commercial breaks, in the new technology, are simple to avoid.

The answer is that advertisers, and their agencies, are going to have to become cleverer and more inventive at using the new technology.

TPS in France has been offering interactive advertising for the last two years, giving it more experience of this kind of marketing than any other company in the world. They have adopted a means of referring to the presence of adverts, so that viewers don't have to see them at a particular time but can go to them when they are ready.

This is, of course, anathema to traditional television advertisers who like the element of compulsion imposed by siting adverts in a gap in the middle of a programme. However, TPS recognizes that successful adverts on a digital television service have to try harder to attract attention, and therefore it runs adverts which give a higher level of added benefits to its viewers.

For example, Renault have used TPS's system to advertise the Kangoo, a people-carrier which they recently launched. Instead of merely running a simple 30-second slot for the Kangoo, TPS arranged for short references on its channels and interactive services that there was a Kangoo waiting to be test driven by the viewer at his or her local dealer. Intrigued, viewers went to an interactive advertisement (accessible at any time) which named their local Kangoo dealer and allowed them to arrange a time for a test drive. It was in effect, a national campaign which was executed entirely locally.

TPS was amazed by the level of the response to this advert. Ten per cent responded to it but even this statistic is misleading. In fact, 10% *of all subscribers* to the channel requested a test drive, giving it a response rate much higher than most forms of direct mail. Clearly, if interactive advertising gives enough of a benefit to the new viewer, they will pay *more* attention than they do to traditional advertising.

So far we have only looked at what will be available from 2001. A couple of years from now intelligent set-top boxes will roll out on cable and satellite systems around the world, allowing even more innovative forms of advertising. Take the Future TV system, which is on test at the time of writing in both Spain and Ireland. This has artificial intelligence within its set-top box which tracks which programmes viewers watch and then suggests programmes which it believes a user would like to see next. In effect, it constructs a personal TV channel for the viewer.

This kind of personalization is not entirely new – Amazon.com uses a similar system to suggest new books in which the reader might be interested. However, it is new to television, and television is likely to go this route for one simple, compelling reason; it is switching over to video on demand.

Video on demand provides viewers with access to a library of thousands of television programmes all ready to play exactly when the viewer wants them. This creates a dilemma for viewers, as they haven't the time or inclination to surf thousands of television programmes looking for a programme they want to watch. Some form of selection tool has to be used, rather like an internet search engine. These selection tools are likely to monitor both programming and buying preferences, keeping a record of what the viewer shops for on the system as much as what he or she watches.

This will allow the viewer to receive personal advertising messages, but they are unlikely to look like present-day advertisements. If the TV knows about the viewer, it can tease or intrigue them with more flair and alacrity than the TV of the 1960s.

Future TV, for example, is proposing that avatars (computer-generated people) pop up on the screen when the viewer is looking for programmes to watch and lead the user to special product offers designed particularly for him or her.

Digital television hands power decisively to the viewer. Advertisers will no longer be able to rely on the viewer's attention or to assume that that viewer is watching, when in reality they aren't. Digital television systems will be able to detect advertising which isn't being watched. Spending on creating and building brands will switch away from the 30-second slot to new, innovative types of advertising which viewers will watch because they are intriguing, clever and benefit the viewer, and not because advertising can't be avoided.

This will cause a major challenge and change in the advertising industry and in the way in which they think about branding and marketing.

CHECKPOINTS

■ Always think about the values that underpin your service and devise a series of emotional reasons why people would want to use your product.

■ Think of your online company as a service which doesn't use technology. How would you describe its benefits to your target audience? This will prevent you from describing your service in terms of technology which is opaque to most people.

■ Always think of the emotional reasons your target audience has for using your service and do not get distracted by the opinions of people like yourself (unless they are your target market).

■ See if there are any online techniques you can use to reinforce your brand. Online has huge potential for brand building and reinforcement.

CHAPTER 7

The Plan and the Pitch

The work put into the planning and presentation of an online business to potential investors will make all the difference between obtaining funding and partners or living with a lost dream. It is incredible how many aspiring entrepreneurs go into meetings with potential investors lacking even the basics of how to present both themselves and their business. Online businesses do differ in some respects from how a traditional business should be presented. There are technology issues in online which traditional businesses often don't have to address and, nine times out of ten, online propositions and opportunities are unfamiliar to traditional investors. This chapter goes through the dos and don'ts of presentation and provides a framework for laying out an online business plan.

Don't do this

If you think a lot of what you read about business presentation is common sense, then consider what happens in the real world. Investors will inevitably ask probing questions (after all, they are risking their money) and an entrepreneur has to be ready for that. However, it is still possible to witness presentations in which entrepreneurs:

- Do not really know where their revenues will come from

- Are unable to justify the pricing of their products

- Demand a new amount of money by next week or the business will close

- Are uncertain whether they have obtained licences or rights to software

▓ Are unable to explain their figures or the exact investment required.

It is unlikely that such a lack of knowledge about a proposed venture will impress an investor and therefore these kinds of presentation don't get funded.

Do this

It is impossible to work out every detail of an online business before looking for funds. In fact no one will know if the business plan works until the business is up and running and intelligent investors know this. Therefore the important thing when preparing what you should say in a presentation is to ensure that the key information that investors need is well presented and thought through.

However, it is acceptable to walk into a presentation to investors without:

▓ Having built the necessary software (or being entirely sure which method you will use to construct it)

▓ Knowing precisely who the management team will be

▓ Having fully researched the market demand for your products

▓ Having other business and investment partners lined up.

Of course it is far better to have done these things but not essential. What investors really want to hear about an online business can be illustrated through a template of headings which you ought to have in your plan and which are detailed later in this chapter. However, filling out a template and turning up with it to a presentation ignores the most important element of presenting anything and that is the way in which you communicate to your audience. This is a psychological issue, and should be at the front of your mind when writing and presenting a business case.

The two-minute rule

A business plan presentation constructed by one of the big firms of management consultants (which grew, generally, out of accountancy businesses) tends to have two fatal flaws:

▪ It is too long

▪ It fails to hold the listener's attention.

The second of these is the worst, as often presentations simply feel too long because they don't hold your attention.

Most business plan presentations fail to take into account the *two-minute rule*, which states that most human beings make a judgement about you and what you are saying within the first two minutes of meeting you. It is not impossible to change someone's mind after that, although it takes a great deal of time and effort.

Why do humans make snap judgements about people? Psychologists believe that it dates from when we were hunters and had to assess a dangerous situation quickly: 'is this unknown person trustworthy and should I therefore ignore that spear he is carrying?' However, it is absolutely the wrong reflex to possess when it comes to assessing management or business plans which requires clear, deliberate cool thought. But as no one has managed to unprogramme this reflex, we are stuck with it.

So the answer is to use it to your advantage. If people make an irrational judgement within the first two minutes of a meeting, exploit it. The movie business uses this often, the first two minutes of most movies are designed to hold you. If they don't, boredom will set in (or worse, you will change TV channel).

The easiest way to do this is to condense what you want to say down to just three (or even better, two) important ideas. *Then make sure you promote them within the first two minutes of the presentation.* Never go above three. Research has shown that the maximum number of ideas which people absorb and retain in half an hour is just three. In the advertising industry, where they know they have got your attention for only seconds, the great practitioners reduce the number of ideas to just one. Hence in 1979, the Tory posters (designed by Saatchi and Saatchi) summed up a complex series of discontents with the Labour government with the slogan 'Labour isn't working'.

The second important element in exploiting the two-minute rule is based on another advertising idea that if you want to tell someone something, you must first get their attention. Companies are often hesitant about taking this advice and say: 'but we are presenting to some stuffy merchant bankers'. However, there are many ways of drawing attention to a business plan which do not involve wearing red noses and antlers. Attention seeking is a legitimate tactic, as the stuffy bankers are also humans and they will like and remember you.

The art in all this is to work out the three most appealing aspects of your business and how to present them in an arresting way within the first two minutes. To do this requires discipline and a method. The method is simple and can be summarized as follows:

Identify the important elements of your business

Reduce the business to its three most important ideas

Identify a way of drawing attention to these ideas

Construct the presentation to start with the three ideas

Reiterate the ideas throughout the presentation
and use them to make it arresting

The first step, identifying the important elements of your business, is the most exacting and requires most work. Get this right and the rest is simply creativity and flair.

The first step

Identifying the most important elements of your business is best done by listing a number of headings and analysing the business according to each one. Even though you may not use this format to construct your presentation, it is useful to be able to write a paper with the business presented in this way so that you can give it to your backers as a follow-up to the main pitch. That way you know that you've covered all the main questions they would like answered.

The headings which are best to use with an online business are slightly different from those of a conventional business plan. This is because it is useful to capture assets which are peculiar to online trading but are not so important in traditional businesses. These are:

- Opportunity

- Market context

- Management
- Assets
- Barriers to entry
- Development plan
- Strengths
- Risks
- Financials.

These are now discussed in more detail.

Opportunity

The opportunity should set out very briefly why the company thinks it can make money in the market in which it intends to operate. In its original plan, Amazon.com might have said that the company thinks that the book market is ideal for a global online service provider, as those who buy books are early adopters of the internet and are happy to mail order online as long as they can get their book delivered in 48 hours. Amazon would then need to point out that it has secured the people and software to create such a service.

Market context

The market context gives an account of the present state of the market in which you are competing and why it is ready for your initiative. This is a good place to give any statistics you have obtained which support your view of that market.

Doing Amazon's original plan you would need to show that there is sufficient discontent among existing book buyers that they would like to do business online and that many of the discontents are online already or are likely to be. It would also be useful to show, as a headline, how the existing book trade has high overheads which Amazon could undercut through trading online. This is probably what Amazon emphasized in its business plan, hence discounting is still a strong feature of its service. However, it no longer needs to discount heavily, such are the obvious benefits of its search facilities, its vast stock of books and its rapid delivery service. At the time of the original plan, these benefits would not have been seen as so significant. But the original business benefits, as expressed in a plan, often define a service for many years to come.

Management

Unlike other business plans, online businesses are very dependent for funding on the quality of their management. In fact, investors often say that they only look at the quality of the management, because if the business goes wrong then good management will anticipate problems and correct them. This is particularly important in markets which are unfamiliar and uncharted, with investor and management no wiser whether there is a real opportunity there.

It is not necessary, before funding, to have a complete management team in place, one or two individuals with promising track records should suffice.

It might be useful to have technologists on the team but they are not vital. It is more important to have a team with a track record of running a business in a disciplined way. Investors will be looking for evidence that you have actually made a difference to a business in which you have worked, particularly in difficult circumstances. Therefore, members of a management team should ideally feature three things which they have done which brought a business profit or value. The fact that they were responsible for appraising 150 people in a bureaucracy is not very credible. Also beware of former consultants, who seemed to feature large in the first wave of dot.com start-ups. Consultants consult, and rarely have hands-on experience of running a business, especially when the going gets tough. That is what is needed in an online start-up – people who keep their nerve and focus under pressure. If your team have worked and achieved in those circumstances, try to show this off to your best advantage in the business plan.

Do you need a CEO at the start? The answer is not necessarily but you do need a team leader – someone who will make the final decision when it comes to disputes. The circumstances in which a CEO is best appointed later are when no one member of the team feels that they have the right experience. If you have a number of brilliant technologists and salespeople, then it makes sense to say to investors: 'look at the strength of this team but we need someone who has actually run a business'.

Tim Jackson, for example, put together the team for the online auction house QXL.com and raised a formidable amount of capital from Apax partners. However, he did not nominate himself as CEO as he believed his experience (as a journalist) was not sufficiently relevant. Often investors are impressed if you have made these judgements in advance of your presentation.

Assets

This is not a headline which appears near the front of conventional business plans but it is very important in online, as it describes things which are peculiar to an online business and are important to its worth.

The simplest form of asset is a deal with an existing player to hire or use their facilities, such as the one between Toys R Us and Amazon, where Amazon uses their stock and Toys R Us uses their home delivery service.

However, the two most valuable assets an online business can possess are its software and information on customers. It is likely that, at the financing stage, the software is not built and the database required to accumulate customer information is just a paper dream. However, if your business is going to end up with these kind of assets, it is worth making a point of it as software and information which is owned:

   Creates barriers to entry by other players (as they will have to go to the expense of developing their own software to compete with your business)

   Accumulates in value if the business succeeds and makes it possible to license these assets to third parties.

A good example of this is Yahoo! who own the rights to their search software. However, they have little information on their users as they do not sell directly to them. Amazon has large databases of information on what people have bought from it over the years and this is immensely valuable commercially.

Software is not as straightforward as this, of course. Even proprietary bits of software often run on existing applications such as database software. In this case it is worth stating what is your own (or will be your own) and what licences (on what terms) you have obtained for the applications. Licensing is becoming very complex, with individual licences required, for example, for running certain off the shelf applications over the internet. Details on these points will impress potential investors.

Unless you come to an agreement with a software house that the software they are developing on your behalf is yours, they will assume that it is theirs. Many software houses reserve the rights to *any* software developed by them. If they do, go elsewhere. It is worth paying more for exclusive rights as they could become a large part of the value of your business, particularly if you are forced into receivership.

If you intend to develop software, it is worth commissioning a demonstration of what it will look like when it is working. There are techniques now, such as rapid application development (RAD), which allow the easy creation of a number of demonstration screens. Although this merely imitates the software, as the full 'back end' has not been built, it is a highly effective way of selling investors a product. Most investors do not understand software and are not able to imagine how a product will work from a paper description. A demonstration is far more effective. However, do make it clear to them that it is only a demonstration and that you will need the investment to make it work.

Barriers to entry

Think about whether there are any barriers to others entering your market. The criticism of many online start-ups is that there are few barriers to entry (certainly something which has been levelled against lastminute.com, which does not own any software of its own and relies for its competitive advantage on doing cheap ticket deals faster than any other online operator).

Online businesses often have entry barriers which are not immediately obvious. For example, anyone is free to start their own digital satellite television service in the UK (or anywhere else). However, you will have to acquire:

- Satellite rights to movies and programmes

- A software system which decodes material to which subscribers are entitled

- A licence to use a satellite for transmitting material

- Customer receiving equipment and install it in five million customers' homes.

In order to compete head on with SkyDigital, you would have to match them item for item on this list. In fact only one of them is proprietary (the software) but an alternative system could be written for you, or even licensed. Want to try? Of course not – as you would have to spend many millions of pounds (as Sky has already done). But all these are barriers to entry (the main barrier they create being expense).

It is always worth saying what the barriers to competing with you are and it may be something as simple as having the only people who understand a particular market or technology.

Development plan

The development schedule is essential to online business plans. An online business normally requires some degree of development before it is ready to trade. This could be as complex as creating a piece of software and researching and creating a product set. Many start-ups can take as long as nine months researching a series of products and then going back to the software developers to tell them to change course. This part of the process cannot be rushed. Significantly, this means spending money ahead of any prospect of income.

So software businesses need a plan. Microsoft Project is a good application for laying out a development schedule (Figure 7.1). This uses critical

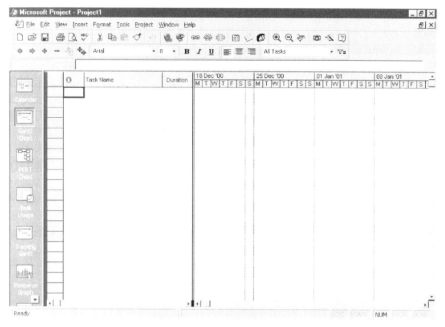

Figure 7.1 Microsoft Project can be used to create a development plan

path analysis which is a way of ensuring that, while you can do various tasks at the same time, you don't start one task before finishing another on which it is dependent.

The advantage of this information is that it gives investors a sense of how much time the development phase will take. Of course it also gives them a timetable to which they can hold the entrepreneur if they invest in the business.

Strengths

You should always examine the competitive advantages of your proposal. Michael Porter is a Harvard Business School professor who has done a lot of work on competitive advantage and he declares that profitability is determined by 'whether firms can capture the value they create for their customers, or whether this value is competed away to others'.[1] In other words, the crucial question for any new business is not whether you have an advantage but whether you can hang onto it. If you can, you will remain profitable.

This sustainable advantage is determined by your innate strengths. Normally this means your management team, and possibly some deals and software which are exclusive to you. However, a point which many entrepreneurs miss is that to sustain your advantage you have to invest in it. One method is familiar to all entrepreneurs; to hold on to a talented management team you have to give them shares or options. This has the advantage of both giving them wealth and locking them into your business. However, if you have an advantage in the form of a unique piece of software, you will also have to invest in it to sustain your advantage over the competition. Technology never stands still. A senior manager at the BBC once said that it now had the right technology to last it the next ten years. He didn't realize that he wasn't in the sufficiency business, he was in the competition business. To sustain advantage you have to keep moving forward and that means a steady investment in whatever gives you advantage now.

Therefore you need to spell out your business's strengths, particularly how you will sustain them.

Risks

Never leave out the risks to a business strategy in your business plan. Plans which somehow forget to include them show a lack of perspective and a lack of awareness of the competitive environment. If you lack those, you will not make sensible business decisions.

However, don't use this headline to demolish the basis of your plan. Keep to things which could go wrong but are manageable, such as slippage in the delivery dates of software or long lead times in the signing of contracts (a particular risk if your clients are public sector organizations).

Financials

Which figures you should calculate and why you should quote them are all laid out in the next chapter. However, if there are any which are very large or seem to grow unrealistically fast (particularly revenue), take a look at them carefully and work out how you will explain them. Seasoned investors have an alarming habit of glancing at the financial section of a proposal and picking out an odd figure and asking for an explanation. You need to be ready with one.

The next steps

If you fully analyse your online idea using all these headings, you will know far more about it than it is wise or interesting to tell a potential investor at a first meeting. Remember the two-minute rule!

Write up the analysis as a report and give it to them after your presentation. Don't do it before or during as some investors have an annoying habit of referring to the greater level of detail in it and picking holes in it. This is a common human characteristic called 'showing off to peers'. Don't encourage it, leave the detailed plan behind so when the pedants see it they no longer have an audience.

How do you reduce all this to just three ideas? The best discipline is to look at the products you are proposing to sell and ask 'what benefits do these give to the customer?'

This is a defining moment, particularly with engineering driven propositions, as often these businesses are purely constructed to satisfy the vanity of the inventor. One business looking for funding was based on a piece of software which could turn web-based information into a format where it could be used on WAP-enabled mobile phones. It was a clever piece of software, until you discovered that it was quicker and easier for mobile phone companies to buy the information at source, in whatever form it came, than it was to get it second hand from a website. The company was, in effect, a showroom for the skills of a technologist and conferred little benefit whatsoever on its potential customers.

Pure fiction

Let's take a fictional example of an online proposition which has been set up to exploit the demand of the Blair government in the UK that all local councils must be capable of receiving online payments for their various services by 2005. We'll call the business 'Future Payments'.

It has a *management team* comprising:

Steve Hurricane – a salesman with a good track record in the publishing industry. He has various awards for selling more copies of the authorized biography of Richard Branson than anyone else in the world.

Rick Danger – a technologist who specializes in databases, particularly in copying and mirroring the contents of databases. He has managed to reproduce and sort out all the product details of a shambolic Belgian electronics company by capturing them from hundreds of company websites around the world where they were arranged by the divisions that made them and not by anything which was logical to a customer.

Trixie Correct – has contacts with many local councils and is seen as a 'thought leader' in e-commerce by the Labour government. She has an MBA from Bradford Management Centre. She is down as chief executive.

What happens to the proposal when it is described under the 'online headlines'?

Opportunity

The opportunity is provided by the statutory requirement of the Labour government demanding that all council bills are available and payable online by 2005. Anyone who can come up with a reasonably priced solution to this problem should find a market, as there are over 600 councils in the UK.

Market context

The fact is that most of these councils are strapped for cash and transferring information from one database to another is a complex business. Most software solutions to this problem will be expensive and could be unreliable. Even the smallest councils have 100,000 residents and the challenge is to get all their payment records onto the web so that they are secure, confidential and up to date. Equally important, most councils have different database systems built at different times to different specifications.

Assets

Future Payments (FP) intends to construct its own software which will enable it to present bills reliably and confidentially. To do this it is going to use the experience of Rick Danger who is a wizard at creating a database which mirrors and updates information from an existing one. This information can then be manipulated by the bill presentation software which FP intends to build. Both the database copying and the billing software will be owned by FP.

Barriers to entry

These are quite straightforward, the management team and the software. Any competitor will have to create a team with Trixie's contacts and Rick's expertise and the ability to commission proprietary software. Also the software (which will take six months to build) will give FP a head start.

Development plan

Rick has drawn up a detailed development plan which shows that, from the point it starts trading, it will take FP nine months before it makes its first sale. This is useful as it holds FP to a timetable and FP essentially contracts with investors that it will deliver revenue on this timescale.

Strengths

The strength of the proposition is that here is a market which has been created by statute and there are few companies capable of serving it right now. The timescale is short (four years) and it looks as though most councils will struggle to fulfil it. The combination of council and software expertise is rare, and FP possesses it. Crucially, Rick's solution gets around one of the most difficult challenges – that different councils hold data on a number of different systems, and nothing is standardized.

The software to be developed belongs to FP and to FP alone. It is also worth noting that this is a business to business application and therefore doesn't require the huge marketing costs of business to consumer propositions.

Also once a council is signed up it will be hard (as long as the software delivers) to get rid of FP as the council will be dependent on its system.

Risks

Councils, being public sector, tend to take longer than commercial organizations to make decisions. This means that signed contracts are likely to come through more slowly than in the commercial sector. However, the FP financial plan has made allowances for this.

There is a risk that the timetable for developing the software might slip but Rick is used to large software development projects and thinks it is manageable. The team also needs to recruit a finance director, a marketing manager and a couple more salespeople.

Financials

The financials show an investment requirement of £5 million and an internal rate of return in the first ten years of 25% (see next chapter). This is a relatively low investment requirement and a decent (although not astronomic) internal rate of return (IRR). However, it is an inexpensive way of buying a captive market. And once a market is captured profit margins can be very tasty (ask Bill Gates).

Reducing it all to three ideas

FP is heavily dependent for its competitive advantage on database software which allows Rick to pull data off a number of different systems run by different councils and reformat it into a state where his software can handle it. In fact this is, in many ways, the unique selling proposition of FP and it is the reason that they can meet councils' needs at a reasonable price ahead of any competition.

However, it is a difficult idea to sell to the average investor as it involves promoting something called 'middleware'. Middleware is software which sits between two other pieces of software and usually transfers information between the two (which indeed is the case here). However, it is rather like trying to sell IBM 370s to the owners of Playboy. Investors simply can't see why it is relevant.

So we have to look for benefits to councils and investors. These are:

- Inexpensive billing software for councils

- Unique expertise in council systems and requirements

- Software which will set a standard and capture a large chunk of a market which is being forced online by statute.

If you were looking for a tag to the FP brand (aimed at councils) it might be:

The future is clear. Here is an affordable way of reaching it.

This combines the two important ideas of a future which the government says councils must achieve and the idea that here is something *affordable and reliable* to which their budgets can stretch.

To construct a presentation it would be worth mocking up a screen which shows the individual bill payment page of the potential investors to whom you are presenting with their council's logo on it. Anything which involves paying money online usually engages even stuffy investment bankers. *They will remember you.* On it (and throughout the presentation) use the date 2005 on all powerpoint pages to emphasize the fact that this has to happen by a deadline. It reinforces the idea of a future which the councils must fulfil and also that here is the software to do it.

Another way of promoting the proposal to investors is to show the difference between paying local charges in Birmingham, Michigan and Birmingham, UK. It will become crystal clear that, with the percentage of internet users in the UK fast approaching the percentage in the US, it is inevitable that UK residents will soon demand that they can pay online and, what's more, *the UK government is demanding it by 2005.*

These are the ideas to reiterate throughout a short presentation. The best business plans are no longer than four pages, short, to the point and with the important issues about the business thought through and addressed. Detail is for the accountants. Clear ideas are for shrewd investors.

CHECKPOINTS

- Remember the two-minute rule – everyone is wired to judge other people and their ideas within two minutes.

- Exploit the two-minute rule by getting over the most important two or three ideas about your business within the first two minutes of your presentation.

- Be able to answer what comes under the following headings when pitching to potential investors:

  - Opportunity

  - Market context

  - Management

  - Assets

  - Barriers to entry

  - Development plan

  - Strengths

  - Risks

  - Financials.

- However, only submit a report using these headings on paper after your presentation. Use this method to construct your presentation:

  - Identify the important elements of your business

  - Reduce the business to its three most important ideas

  - Identify a way of drawing attention to these ideas

  - Construct the presentation to start with the three ideas

  - Reiterate the ideas throughout the presentation and use them to make it interesting.

CHAPTER 8

Doing the Numbers

All online ventures are start-ups. There was nothing like them before so they have to be built from scratch. That means they need financing in some way. Financiers demand business plans of some type before they invest money in a company, normally to convince themselves that they are not investing in a non-runner. This chapter deals with current thinking about the financing and financial performance of online start-ups.

There was, at the beginning of the year 2000, a belief that online ventures were in some way different from all businesses that had gone before. Some commentators believed that new economy companies didn't have to turn a profit for years because they would produce such obvious, instant changes to the way in which people do business that it would be clear that they contained immense, innate value. So their value would rise forever on the stock market without the need for profitability. This came to a grinding halt when some dot.coms ran out of cash, essentially because they had not been making a profit. It then dawned on the market that many more might run out of cash before ever producing any value. Investors also began to remember that old business metric which shows that, of all start-ups, only 20% ever succeed. Then they realized that this rule probably also applied to online ventures.

The net effect of all these revelations is that investors are much more wary about dot.coms. There is a joke in the City of London that only a fool believes that old-fashioned paper won't be replaced in the new electronic age and that is why investors no longer accept worthless paper[1] from dot.com start-ups. This is the kind of thing which amuses financiers.

However, it is important not be laughed at when you go looking for money for your online venture, if only for your morale. The most important thing is to produce a set of figures which will pass the financier test and to do that you have to know what worries financiers. Most consultants can advise an entrepreneur of this. If a consultant is asked 'Are the figures consultants believe in and the figures that will convince a financier the same?', I'm afraid the answer is 'No'. However, the entrepreneur needs to be aware where he or she has taken liberties with the presentation of the figures and to know where those risks are. Because if you come to believe the figures in most business plans you are on the road to ruin.

It would be commendable to submit totally realistic business plans but the truth is that no one else seeking capital does and you won't get financed if you show something close to the real truth. Unfortunately, most online entrepreneurs don't realize the naked truth until they are nine months into a start-up. It is not as if they are lying, it is simply that they fail to appreciate the truth, even though a consultant is normally more than happy to volunteer it. Strangely, many entrepreneurs never ask consultants their opinion, even though they are paying for it.

However, shrewd and seasoned investors are well aware of the liberties taken in business plans and the whole process assumes the nature of an elaborate game. So what goes through the mind of an experienced venture capitalist when presented with the figures in a business plan? William Rees-Mogg was once editor of *The Times* in London but has since turned to professional investing and has usefully published his thoughts on business plan numbers:

> My own rule of thumb, based on experience, is that forecasts of revenue may be overestimated by 50%, the time taken to build the revenue stream may be underestimated by 50% and the costs may be underestimated by 50% as well. Consequently the cash required to reach fruition may be a multiple of what is provided for in the business plan.[2]

With such thoroughly sceptical investors at large, it is surprising that online enterprises get financed at all, but they do. In fact, when the money from their first stage financing runs out, they often get financed again and again.

Online financial logic

Online financial logic tends to be different from that of traditional businesses, for example an advertising agency or a retailer such as Wal-Mart. The essential difference is that most online businesses have very high start-up costs and then very low costs for expanding the business to a larger and larger customer base. The cost of servicing an extra customer is known as a 'marginal cost', in other words, the additional costs which are incurred when the business has already absorbed the costs of starting up the enterprise.

The reason for this is that most online businesses have to start with a large investment in software and hardware. The basic online business model tends to be a highly centralized transaction and selling operation (often based on a server in one country and selling to many from there). While operations such as distribution and warehousing are sometimes local, the bulk of the assets of an online company are in its content, its agreements with its suppliers and its software. And the software in particular requires a huge upfront investment, often with extra expenditure to get this software just right.

In addition, because many online businesses are new it takes a lot of expenditure on marketing and promotion to get them known. These costs combine to give the early cash flow of an online business or a dot.com a large trough shape in its early years. Therefore it is pointless to search for profits, it is better to look at how quickly the business is moving out of the trough towards making a month on month profit (excluding the debt which this business has already accumulated). This is known as an 'operating profit'.

Tim Jackson started the online auction house QXL.com in Europe. He recently wrote:

> One point is clear. Internet businesses are unusual in often having high fixed costs, often in technology, but low marginal costs. Think of Yahoo!, increasing sales in the space of a year by a factor of 10, but keeping its increase in costs to less than 30%.[3]

This hides a paradox, in that for any business to be successful it has, at some stage, to make a profit and most pure online businesses show little signs of doing so (including Amazon). Can online ever be successful or is it just a wake-up call for traditional businesses who will end up absorbing the lessons of the start-ups and their technology?

The truth is not that simple. It is still too early to tell. I also think that to succeed in online you don't have to be first, you have to be the best (a theme developed elsewhere in this book). However, if the financiers *see you* as best, they will extend to you the financial means to continue your business. For example, BSkyB, one of the boldest digital television enterprises on the planet, has moved from operating loss to profit and back again several times in its first five years but has survived because the financiers have always been prepared to buy more shares in it. Why? Because its products are undoubtedly very good and affordable but also because its management is steered by Rupert Murdoch, whose reputation could finance virtually any media venture he chose to embark upon. Being perceived to be best is important, because perceptions are real and translate into money.

Methods of finance

There are five main ways in which online enterprises are financed in their early years:

- From the cash the company generates

- Borrowing

- Getting an existing company to provide the cash (usually for an equity stake)

- Raising the money from venture capitalists

- Floating on the stock market.

The last two are the most common, but all are used, depending on the type of online business proposed.

Financing the company from the cash it generates

This is almost impossible with a dot.com start-up where the initial expenditure is high compared to the speed at which it generates revenue. It has been done by web design companies, which are essentially selling a service on to the people taking the risk of setting up an online business. The important distinction here is that web design companies operate on the model of service industries, where weightless goods (such as ideas, designs and software) are sold to clients. If you can develop a reputation quickly as a service industry, you can lever that reputation to obtain higher fees and then use them in order to expand. It is a wonderful way to build a business as you end up with little debt and therefore no one dictating what the business should or should not be doing. However, in online this method of finance is almost unknown.

Borrowing

Borrowing is what almost all small businesses used to do before the 1980s in order to get started. They would go to the local bank manager with a business plan and see if they could get a small business loan. It still happens, but took a severe knock in the recession of the early 1980s when there was mass panic among the banks about their exposure to failing companies. Debts were recalled with little or no justification. Entrepreneurs fell out of love with the banks, who have never quite recovered their stature.

The advantage of borrowing is that if you can get it right the company is still yours at the end of the day as you haven't relinquished any ownership in it. However, when companies struggle to repay debt, they often end up giving away chunks of ownership in order to keep lenders satisfied.

Quite often online companies are financed by a combination of equity and borrowing. The owners (who hold the equity) buy a stake and extend money to the company through a loan. The advantage of this is that as the online company makes money the lenders have first call on the profits to repay their debt, making it a quicker method of getting money back than through simply holding equity.

When it comes to standing in line for a share of the profits, equity holders are at the end of a long queue, coming after lenders, the tax man and, in the worst cases, the receivers' fees.

Getting an existing company to provide the cash

There are three established ways of raising money through issuing equity (or shares) and this is the most sensible for start-ups.

Established companies will fund online start-ups if the start-up covers an area of business which the established company would like to enter. For example, Chime plc (the advertising and communications company) has funded ventures in domain registration and online advertising in return for a share in two companies, DomainAudit and Web Marketing.

The advantage for the start-ups is that they get access to the traditional company's expertise, client base, and client network. The investing company also learns about the business of the online start-up, its technology and what customers will and won't buy. Its shares sometimes get a boost from these relationships, although it is not necessarily a one-way street because if the stockmarket panics about dot.coms the investing company's shares can also go down. The most celebrated example of this in the UK is Dixons, who hold an 80% stake in the internet access provider Freeserve. The problem is that the two shares are now linked – with every rumour about Freeserve having a disproportionate effect on Dixon's share price.

The risk in this type of relationship is that dot.coms and older companies are often a bad cultural fit. Dot.coms are often based more on enthusiasm than experience and inhabit a land where profitability is a distant vision. They are often the creation of people with little experience of shareholders who question the profits performance. In these sorts of relationship the profit motive soon catches up with the online start-up and there is either a parting of the ways or an experienced manager is sent in to try and sort out the dot.com. While this can be traumatic, it is often a useful experience for the start-up company.

Venture capital

Venture capitalists do not tend to get a very good press, and anyone selling equity to a venture capitalist has to be clear about their motives. They are not heroes of the new media age or public servants concerned with developing high technology, as their public relations position them. That is not how they make a living. They are there to spot value in small but fast growing companies and invest in them in the hope that they too will increase their money by a very high multiple. They are acutely aware that only one in five companies will do this, therefore they expect several of their investments to return nothing. A venture capitalist has two essential skills:

- Spotting winners

- Working out who is a loser and when to pull the plug on them.

Venture capitalists typically expect returns over three years of 30% a year on their original investment. They normally achieve this through some sort of flotation (in other words, selling shares to the public through a stock exchange). The ordinary investor (unless he or she is very lucky) can normally only dream about these kinds of return. The venture capitalists have to spend a great deal of time networking and spotting and encouraging management talent in order to make successful companies. In fact, seasoned venture capitalists always say that they don't invest in business plans, they invest in people.

The hard part is finding them.

Floating the company

This is the way to make serious money, but it is not without pitfalls, for example most business to consumer dot.coms which were floated recently are now below their issue price (the price at which their shares were originally sold to the public).

It is very difficult (although not impossible) to float a company without a trading record, and this is why most floats are of companies which have been trading for at least a year (although often without making a profit).

The NASDAQ is a very popular market for high technology companies, a market which the German stock exchange, for example, has emulated with the creation of the Neuer Markt. Easier still are markets which have less demanding listing requirements, such as AIM in the UK. However, buyers of these shares have to beware, because AIM companies have had to disclose less information and fulfil less stringent requirements than the companies on the main exchanges.

In order to float you need to engage the services of an investment banker who will handle the float for you (and underwrite it if the market does not to buy enough of the shares on offer). They do all this for a large fee – payable after the float – and normally out of the proceeds.

If you float successfully, you will attract fund managers who will buy shares in your company. Fund managers – whose concern is to make money for the pension funds or thousands of small investors they represent – are getting increasingly vocal. If they don't like your company's performance, they will not hesitate to tell your board. There is a long history of creators of companies being removed to make way for new chief executives. The phrase 'shoot the inventor' has a sweet resonance in the City. They don't mind who created the company, they simply want their returns.

However, if your online start-up gets as far as a float, you are doing well. But after that you will have to do even better, as then you will have shareholders who will want to see their money growing year on year.

Cash flow is king

There has been a lot of debate about the best way of measuring a company's performance. Traditionally it was profits, which are a snapshot of what the company is making over a set time period after costs have been subtracted. There are several problems with this, the first is that profits are notoriously vulnerable to creative accounting (as Terry Smith pointed out in his book *Accounting for Growth*).[4] The second is that for the first years of their existence, online start-ups do not make profits, therefore there has to be another way of measuring how well they are doing. This is normally done by measuring four things:

- Market share

- Revenue growth

- Years from breakeven

- Cash burn.

Two other metrics are also useful, net present value and internal rate of return, which are explained later in this chapter.

To illustrate these points, let's use a real live example, Scoot.com's results for the year ending 1 September 2000. Scoot is an online directory and classified advertising operation and is partly financed by the French utility company Vivendi and by placing 10% of its equity on the stock market.

In these results, it turns out that Scoot's revenues are down and its losses have increased. But the results were well received and the shares rose almost 3 pence to 127 pence. Why was this?

Market share

The first important Scoot metric, its market share, was increasing. Subscriber numbers in the last quarter rose 16% to 23,000. This pleased investors.

Market share is all important to an online enterprise which has yet to make a profit. It indicates that the enterprise is increasing its customer base and therefore the size of the market it is trading in. Cleverly defining a market is vital to online success, as it allows you to present numbers in a favourable light. So, for example, Scoot has defined its market as the *European online directory market*. But at the moment that market is tiny, so any share of it enjoyed by Scoot will be high in percentage terms. Also any forays into Europe will look bold and are sure to enhance market share. Scoot is pursuing that strategy, with plans to launch a service in France and has interests in Belgium and the Netherlands. All that might sound a bit vague but online investors are keen to hear about market expansion plans.

Market share is measured in a number of ways. Many online enterprises operate by taking details from users before they will let them onto their system. Confusingly, although these people often do not pay a subscription, these users are called 'subscribers'. The advantage of subscribers is that the online operation holds all their details and these are a valuable asset. For example, terrestrial television broadcasters, such as ITV, may have a rough idea who watches their programmes but, in contrast, BSkyB knows exactly, because of their subscription database. As online customer management develops, it will be important to be able to engage in interactive dialogue with customers, and to obtain more details on them in order to know what to sell them next and how to retain their loyalty.

Therefore, subscribers are good as you can use online techniques to retain and grow them. However, don't be confused into thinking that subscribers are actually using a website. Quite often people sign up to use an online service and then never use it. Subscriber figures should really show 'active' and 'passive' subscribers, thus making a distinction between registrations and users. Much work in online marketing is the targeting of passive subscribers with messages or e-mails to encourage them to become active. For example, online share trading services tend to have a big gap between active and passive users and much online messaging, extolling the ease of use and cost savings, is carried out in order to persuade people to become active users.

Revenue growth

Revenue news on Scoot was bad, revenues having fallen 38% in the nine months to £8.2 million. It is also worth noting that losses increased from £10.6 million last year to £16.6 million this year. In fact, these figures, which are conventional ways of assessing business performance, are both bad and show the extent to which online investors are mesmerized by less conventional measurements (such as subscriber numbers).

The most important issue, when presenting revenue predictions, is what kind of revenues will your online venture generate. Make sure it is not one which is currently out of favour. For example, online advertising is falling out of fashion at the time of writing as there is a perception that online advertising revenues will collapse. So if 80% of your revenues are based on online advertising (as at Yahoo!), your shares will experience a downturn and any online start-up proposing such a dependency is unlikely to be funded. Yahoo! announced on 12 October 2000 revenue, earnings and page views above expectations. However, analysts were anxious about a predicted reduction in online advertising and were especially influenced by a report from Merrill Lynch on the subject.

A good revenue stream to have is subscription income, where online users actually pay a monthly fee for a service. For example BSkyB has consistently demonstrated that a monthly fee of about £25 for its digital channels can be greatly increased through the addition of pay per view services.

Also good (although not as good as subscription) are captive revenue streams, such as 'ingress'. Ingress describes telephone charge income which reverts to the service which generated it. So, for example, an internet service provider generates income for a telecommunications operator every time a customer logs onto the internet. A cut of this income is normally then allocated to the internet service provider – ingress income. It is a good revenue stream as it increases in direct proportion to the use of the service.

The third good revenue stream is commission on the sale of online goods and services. Auction services, such as QXL.com, are heavily dependent on this. Some e-commerce operations, for example Open (a television-based service which operates on the BSkyB set-top box), charge large fixed fees for using it as a platform (which is a form of e-commerce levy). This is an interesting revenue, as it is in effect a 'first mover' charge, meaning that it is difficult to sell anywhere else over the television as there is a fixed charge for the privilege. It is unlikely to persist as a source of income.

Years from breakeven

For a loss making company this is a crucial measure. It is the answer to the simple question: 'If you are making losses, when are you going to start making profits?' Scoot delighted analysts by announcing that it was going to make a profit 'in the course of 2001' – about six months ahead of analysts' predictions. When a company starts making an 'operating profit' (that is, ignoring its accumulated debt), it is often easier to get rid of the accumulated debt by selling equity or taking out loan stock. The amount of debt generated is closely linked to cash burn.

Cash burn

Cash burn is the thing which frightens off most investors, and is where business plans are most manipulated. It is the rate at which money is consumed on a company's journey to profitability. Obviously the bigger the revenues (as long as costs are kept under control), the lower the cash burn rate. When the company reaches breakeven, the cash burn rate will reach zero. Companies which never make a profit simply burn cash and eventually, unless they can attract new investment, run out of cash.

If a business plan shows tremendous cash burn in the early stages, it will give cause for concern because:

- If there is a flaw in the business, investors will be left nursing heavy losses from early on

- Any failure to bring in revenue will result in losses being greater and more difficult to reverse.

Also, remember the problem of the honest business planner, who will be confronted by an analyst who thinks that any plan is 50% wrong on all major measurements. So they assume that your plan is the same.

That is why most online business plans massage out heavy cash burn by predicting spectacular revenue growth in the early years. An encouraging assessment of why revenue growth will be strong and healthy is the most important area to concentrate on in an online business plan. However, a section on risks should be included, in other words, what could adversely affect the revenue predictions. This ensures that investors have been given all the relevant information.

Scoot's cash burn was about £5 million a quarter. Although revenues had declined, better cost control was predicted to bring a closer breakeven and, by implication, bring cash burn to zero.

The market's verdict on Scoot.com

In the month after Scoot announced its results, the market became badly affected by worries that oil price increases would produce an economic slowdown and that this would badly affect the profitability of any online start-up. Scoot's shares fell from 127 pence in September to just 100 pence by mid-October. Was the market correct and Scoot's original investors wrong? It is hard not to conclude that Scoot's ultimate fate will be determined by market euphoria or the lack of it.

Net present value and the internal rate of return

The ultimate test of any investment is how much money it returns to the pocket of the investor. There is a strong case for simply concentrating on two measurements when presenting business cases. These are the ones which most graphically enable investors to compare the returns they will enjoy in the online venture with those they would get elsewhere (for example putting their money in a building society). They are called net present value (NPV) and the internal rate of return (IRR).

NPV calculates all the cash the business is predicted to make in a finite period (such as five years) and adjusts this cash for inflation over that period. Thus it gives the total amount of cash delivered over the period adjusted to today's prices. This is useful because if an investor has been promised exactly the same amount of money delivered over a shorter period, clearly he or she should put their money into the shorter project. NPV offers a way of making a comparison.

Most modern spreadsheet programmes allow you to turn a cashflow into an NPV. You have to supply what you think the rate of inflation will be over the given period, and the programme works out the correct NPV. Similarly it can also work out the IRR.

The IRR is the average annual rate at which an investment delivers income. The easiest way to think about it is to think of your business as a building society account. If you held money in it for a fixed period (a number of years), what *annual* percentage would the building society have to pay you to deliver an equivalent return to the one your online venture is promising?

The advantage of this is you can stand in front of investors and tell them that they will have to find an investment which can deliver them, say, 40% a year to match this investment. At 15% IRR or under investors tend not to be interested in investing in business proposals. Essentially, this is because that is what their financial managers say they can give them if they simply give the cash to them for investment on the markets (whether they actually do is another matter).

Many companies have an IRR rate, below which they will not invest in a new business proposition. Most companies will tell you what this is before you submit plans to them, and it is probably worth finding out.

Neither of these measures can disguise a business plan which doesn't convince, of course. But they are always worth quoting, as they give a more exact way of comparing your business, if it flies, with other investments.

Online assets: a golden rule for investors

A final point to consider and one which is particularly true of online investments; many of them have valuable assets which are never properly accounted for in business plans. This is important because a business which is creating assets can be sold for many times its profit (or loss) stream.

In other words, even if your business never makes a profit it may still hold such valuable online assets that you can sell it at a considerable return to yourself as owner.

The two most important classes of online assets are subscriber data and intellectual property.

Online companies often generate subscriber data because users have to subscribe and in doing so they surrender all kinds of interesting information about themselves. This can be as simple as your e-mail address and the fact that you have used a particular web service, or it can be details of your purchasing habits. In an online world this information is increasingly valuable, as in online most marketing is aimed at individuals and not at groups of people. Obviously to make marketing to individuals more effective you have to have a lot of data on them.

There have been instances of online businesses going bust and still managing to sell their subscriber data for a large sum. This raises ethical questions, however, and these ethics are complicated by the fact that if someone takes over one going concern using another going concern no one seems to notice or care very much.

Intellectual property is the holy grail of online enterprises. If your company can create a system, or a piece of software, which it owns exclusively, then you are building value as the business takes off. It is possible in online to have businesses which create intellectual property and license it and that is all they do. They create nothing more than ideas and patents. An excellent example of this is ARM plc which patents microchip designs and then licenses them. It does not make the chips. It is currently one of the 100 biggest companies in the UK.

Some dot.coms create software which is proprietary to them and sometimes license it to other dot.coms. Yahoo! does this. All of this creates huge asset value in a business whose assets are essentially intangible.

Possibly the best online businesses to invest in are those where they own their subscriber base and their software. That way if the business plan doesn't work there is still worth left in the business. If the business plan does work, the business will be worth a huge multiple of its projections.

CHECKPOINTS

■ Most online business plans are wildly optimistic.

    ■ As a result it puts you at a severe disadvantage if you submit realistic figures. Most entrepreneurs find this almost impossible to do, however.

■ Unlike traditional businesses, online businesses have large start-up costs but with the additional cost of each additional transaction or customer set very low.

■ There are five ways for an online business to raise money:

    ■ From the cash the company generates

    ■ Borrowing

    ■ Getting an existing company to provide the cash (usually for an equity stake)

    ■ Raising the money from venture capitalists

    ■ Floating on the stock market.

■ Cash flow is the most important financial factor in an online start-up. The main factors which should be monitored are:

    ■ Market share

    ■ Revenue growth

    ■ Years from breakeven

    ■ Cash burn.

■ Online companies have new types of assets which investors should consider:

    ■ Subscriber data

    ■ Intellectual property rights to software or even business processes.

CHAPTER 9

Partnerships

One of the delights of working in online is the online networking party. Coming, as it does, from California it is not to everyone's taste.

The fundamental idea is that people with online ideas meet backers, and backers meet people with ideas. I was a founding member of one in the UK called 'Digital People' which we used to run from the Victorian headquarters of the National Liberal Club in Whitehall. The fundamental idea was that if you had an idea you sat on a seat with a green sticker and if you had money to invest you sat on a seat with a red sticker and between courses you all changed tables.

Events such as these could be the turning point for a start-up business. Looking at the guest list of one dated 21 September 1999 I see that those present included the CEO of lastminute.com (which didn't have any money at the time) and the CEO of e-commerce site E*Trade. Esther Dyson was also there.[1]

At these events headhunters buzz happily about the red and the green chairs offering people unrealistic prospects of future wealth. However, as many of them were about to discover, who backs your business often makes the difference between success and failure. The mistake is to go purely for the money. The kind of backers who dole out money like chocolate drops are the venture capitalists. Although it is hard to argue with an entrepreneur who has just secured $100 million of funding, they should be aware that:

They now work for the venture capitalists – backers investing this amount will call the shots

The venture capitalists will want 30% a year returns by selling the business either to another company or the stock market as soon as possible

- Divergences from business plans will be not be tolerated for long

- 'Long-term' investing does not exist in the venture capital world.

Far better to think about the kind of backers you want and the way in which you want your business to be backed. Besides purely financial backing (which is covered in Chapter 8), there are two other main types which an entrepreneur should explore:

- Strategic partnerships
- Community partnerships.

Both of these work on the principle that investors are tied into you for reasons which are more than purely financial, either because they can learn from you, it improves their strategic spin to the City or it improves their branding and marketing. This means the relationship you have with them is likely to be slightly longer than that you will have with a venture capitalist if you (or the economy) get into difficulties. However, in the end any money extended to you comes with ties. A chairman once told me the real reason he had just taken 30% of a dot.com. Instead of a priceless pearl of marketing wisdom, I was greeted by the words, 'because I want to make a shed-load of money'.

Strategic partnerships

The most common form of strategic partnership is where the other party has a skill you need and don't have. The quid pro quo is that usually the online entrepreneur has to have access to a market which the partner would like to enter but can't, either because it has the wrong brand or the wrong contacts. A good example is Bertlesmann AG, the large German media company, which bought a stake in Napster, the Californian music downloading site with an audience of 38 million teenagers. Similarly, eBay, the auction site, and Disney announced in October 2000 that they were launching a joint Disney auction marketplace, as eBay had the auction software and Disney had the products.

These deals normally involve the partner giving the online start-up cash in some form, either through purchasing an equity stake or in the form of a loan. Much trickier are equity deals for services, where a company which needs a particular service gets it by giving a partner equity in them for services. The problem with these deals is that they can go very wrong for

the partner, as if the online company crashes the partner is left explaining
to shareholders where the lost revenue has gone.

It is usually marketing or software companies which enter these kinds
of arrangement with online start-ups. They normally consume more
management time than the partner anticipates at the beginning of the
relationship.

Community partnerships

Community partnerships are subtler and innate to the nature of online
where many businesses can be seamlessly and electronically connected
without the consumer knowing where one ends and another begins.

Two examples are the tie ups between Expedia and Microsoft Network
where Expedia provides a travel service for Microsoft Network, and
between Homestore.com and AOL where Homestore provides services for
home seekers for AOL subscribers.

However, these are both big established portals. For start-ups these
deals are harder to orchestrate and the typical start-up makes the mistake
of trying to construct too complex and unfocused a community too
quickly. For example a consortium of lawyers, venture capitalists and
marketers came together early in 2000 to form Matchco, a site to which
entrepreneurs could apply for funding and start-up services. Typical of
these ideas, the partners (and the entrepreneurs) paid a subscription to join
in. However, with so many companies involved, and with the proposition
being blurred by offering many different types of service, it was very difficult to manage.

I have never known this type of community business model to work, so
perhaps it is best avoided.

By far the most effective is the global niche community. This works
with companies providing services over the internet which are highly
specialist. On its own, in its own country, the business without the internet
would not have been viable. However, with the internet it is possible to
build a community of customers and suppliers which means that the business can turn a profit.

Examples include Biorobotics, a company which makes machines
which analyse DNA samples. It is based in Cambridge but its community
is international.

Even stranger is a company which venture capitalists Amadeus backed
which worked out a way of 'rendering' the graphic skeletons which
computer animators use to create characters in films such as *Toy Story*.

Rendering is the process whereby a skeleton is given substance by determining the way in which light would fall on it. Amadeus backed a Cambridge-based company which claimed that it could render an entire movie in 24 hours. They announced this on their website.

The computer animation industry in Cambridge is, in fact, non-existent. However, due to linking to other websites and the tireless robotic search engines used by the animation industry, a group of bankers in St Louis rang up within seven days and asked if they could invest in the company. Even stranger was the next call, which was from Pixar, the makers of *Toy Story*, in California. They said that rendering could not possibly be done at this speed but, just in case they had found a way of doing it, they were sending two plane tickets to California.

This is an eternal and important message in online marketing and partnership, think specialist and think global. Now you can do both.

CHECKPOINTS

■ Consider venture capital with great care. Does it give you anything more than money?

■ Always try and find a partner who will give you experience or a network which you haven't got yourself.

■ Community partnership can be very powerful if you think specialized and think global. Avoid fuzzy, broad partnerships as they rarely work.

CHAPTER 10

The Where

One of the great delights of working in online is watching the huge difficulties it is causing the world's taxmen.

The fact is that e-commerce, where consumers are able to buy goods from other countries over the internet, contains within it the death knell of taxes which have been with us since the Roman Empire. In fact, the impact of online is now acknowledged to be such a problem that both the UK and the US Treasuries are reported to be examining new ways of raising taxation. Both are concerned that corporation tax and income tax will become so easy to avoid that they will become completely untenable.

It appears that hardly any online entrepreneurs consider the importance of where their online business is located. Location, in online, is a very flexible concept. The entrepreneur rarely has to be anywhere near the part of the business where transactions take place. Locating the guts of an online business in the correct place can at least halve, and in some cases eliminate, your tax liability. So where and how you set up your online business can easily make the difference between success and failure.

Taxing the taxman

Take the simple example of VAT. If a US company sells goods over the internet to buyers in Europe, do buyers pay VAT? Brussels says that they should, asking all companies who sell to the EU, wherever they are based, to register for VAT at 15% and to report sales to EU domiciled citizens to the appropriate authorities.

But the US authorities say that sellers shouldn't comply. The US State Department has reacted angrily to the Brussels ruling saying: 'The right to levy tax on American entities is a privilege reserved for Congress.'[1] The US also points out that sellers of online software have no idea where buyers are domiciled, they only have a computer address. And computers can move around (as anyone who has sat on a plane next to a neurotic laptop junkie can tell you). US chip giant Intel suspects it is an EU plot to buy themselves time: 'e-protectionism' they shout.

Corporation tax is an even thornier issue. Where a company is taxed is normally defined by two main criteria; where the business is based and whether the activity there is core to the business. This is known as the 'permanent establishment' of the company. In the case of an online company involved in selling software downloads (such as www.real.com, for example), the core part of the business is processing transactions and streaming out software from a server, which can be done from anywhere in the world. It could as easily be done from a tax haven. A computer in a tax haven is 'permanent', in the sense that it is attached to the internet there. However, all the records of the transactions could easily be moved to a computer somewhere else at the touch of a button.

So the company's core is highly transportable. Well, say the international tax authorities, that is all very well but we know where transactions are performed because invoices are issued and cheques are signed, and surely signatures and cheques will establish a trail which shows us where and how the deals are being done.

But soon most businesses will trade using digital signatures (which governments are rapidly passing into legislation as legally binding). These signatures can exist permanently in a computer *but can be activated remotely*. This means, in short, that companies will be able to conclude a deal in a territory without ever having to be there physically.

Add to that the ability to move records or deals, and digital signatures, from territory to territory and you get the birth of a new phenomenon, 'electronic tax shopping'.

e-tax shopping is simple but devastating for countries with high corporate tax rates. It means that as soon as the corporate tax environment becomes unfriendly in one area, companies will simply move their businesses by flicking them across to a computer in a friendlier regime.

Whole chunks of major companies' internal ordering are now being diverted via the web. This is called 'e-procurement', and it is estimated it will account for $1.3 billion worth of trade by 2003.

If you were a major company (and everyone, from the chemical to the car industries, has announced plans for e-procurement systems), it would make sense to base your e-procurement presence in a computer in a tax friendly place. In other words, to give it a permanent establishment in a competitive tax regime, and to construct it in such a way that it could be moved easily.

The effect of these instantly transportable e-procurement companies is that countries will have to compete to keep e-procurement revenue flows, unless the world's governments can agree on a policy on these virtual permanent establishments.

That seems unlikely to happen quickly. The UK authorities say that 'The government is working with its international partners to clarify the interpretation of the "permanent establishment" concept'.[2]

In fact some tax lawyers are now playing with the idea of servers which are entirely extraterritorial, sitting in outer space or on the bed of the ocean. Under which tax regime do sites based on these stateless servers fall? Under the whim of the owner, argue the lawyers. And which entrepreneur in the world, given the choice, is going to charge themselves tax?

What to look for in an online tax haven

In the absence of stateless servers (at the present time) where is it best to locate an online company? There are five criteria:

- A low tax regime

- Good, large and affordable bandwidth connections to major telecoms spines

- Skilled and affordable technicians to maintain the servers

- A stable political regime

- Security of data and transmission.

A low tax regime

It is worth understanding a bit about tax. As the first section of this chapter demonstrated, the world's tax authorities normally use the idea of a permanent establishment of a company to define where it should pay tax.

Online muddies this as it is possible to argue that the only permanent thing about an online company is where its servers are located. In fact, some states are now considering declaring positively that where the servers are located is where the company is located for tax purposes and waiting for other countries to challenge them. Needless to say these states are outside the EU.

Any state is free to set a corporation tax rate at any level they like. The UK sets it at 30%, Guernsey at 20%. That means that, very simply, it is more worthwhile to establish an online enterprise on Guernsey than in the UK.[3]

However, things are not that simple. For example, there is no VAT in Guernsey (they are not members of the EU), therefore any web user (anywhere in the world) buying from a site in Guernsey shouldn't pay VAT on their purchase, in theory. This means that you can sell goods via the internet from Guernsey for less than if your server was in a state which charges VAT.

Also certain companies are subject to strange and irregular taxes. Gambling companies in the UK suffer a special tax. With the introduction of online gambling a visionary called Victor Chandler set up an online gaming operation in Gibraltar which didn't charge gambling tax. This phenomenon then spread rapidly to Malta, where a whole series of gambling companies are establishing themselves under the watchful eye of Malta's financial regulator, the MSFC.

In the US the situation is even more extraordinary. The Telephone Acts prohibit telephone gambling and are currently being interpreted to include internet gambling. So all online gambling is offshore, chiefly in strange places like Curaçao. But US legislators are also arguing that even offshore gambling should not be allowed, so that Curaçao's money spinner should also be closed down. Quite how they intend to enforce this is not clear at this time.

However, online operations are beginning to relocate to the most favourable tax regime and there is nothing governments can do to stop them. At the moment all governments can do about online tax is bluster and then compromise. In fact, places such as the Channel Islands are struggling to install enough server capacity to meet the demand.

In some places online companies can get very close to paying no tax at all. This is because most of the traditional tax havens have a status which they describe as something akin to an 'international trading company'. This means that the company concerned must have all its directors domiciled abroad and must trade offshore. This, in some jurisdictions, results in an effective rate of corporation tax of 4.12%. This is already being applied to online companies in these jurisdictions.

However, it is not as simple as setting up in an offshore haven. You will have to make sure that they have the infrastructure to support an online business. The final four criteria deal with infrastructure. If your preferred tax haven doesn't possess these do not set up there as it could well prove to be too difficult.

Good, large and affordable bandwidth connections

This is almost the most important infrastructure requirement. If your servers can't connect to the internet at a reasonable cost, you are better off back at home.

There are some huge differences between the amounts charged for bandwidth onto the internet (which online companies buy in bulk, normally in chunks of 2 megabytes/second). Table 10.1 shows that, despite its attractive tax regime, Ireland lagged well behind other countries in terms of its bandwidth costs at the beginning of 2000.

It is, of course, no accident that the US has stimulated such rapid growth in online services with bandwidth costs as low as 312 euros/month for 2 megs/sec. Cheap bandwidth encourages online start-ups.

The main reason for cheap bandwidth is competition among telecoms providers. It is amazing how cheap bandwidth becomes when there's someone down the road selling it for less. Left to their own devices, telecoms operators will charge anything for bandwidth – and usually do – arguing that they will sell cheap as long as the internet service provider buys in bulk. This is a spurious argument, as they would do far more to stimulate use and growth if they sold cheap. But telecoms giants never seem to think in this way.

The problem is that in many tax havens they haven't yet liberalized their telecommunications regime which means that there is a telecom monopoly. This always leads to high bandwidth prices. In fact in the case of one island the monopoly telecoms company was charging 31,600 euros/month for 2 megs/sec. As a result online activity was severely stunted.

So the first question you should always ask when you get off the plane in your tax haven is: 'what are the bandwidth charges?'

Table 10.1 Comparison of international bandwidth costs

Country	Cost in euros/month for 2 megs/sec bandwidth (Jan 2000)
Ireland	1600
Spain	1000
France	1000
Italy	1000
UK	600
Germany	500
Finland	390
USA	312

Skilled and affordable technicians to maintain the servers

Many tax havens have great difficulty creating the correct skills base for online. That is why server firms in tax havens can charge a premium rate, they have cornered the local talent.

Many tax havens have very strict immigration controls, put in place to stop people flooding in to take advantage of low taxes. However, it is proving a hindrance to companies who want to recruit the appropriate skills. It is said that US investors, before deciding to invest in Europe, always ask how easy it is to sack an employee. In tax havens it is necessary to ask how easy it is to recruit one.

Always check out the storage and maintenance charges for hosting your site in another country to see if you will make a net gain from relocating.

A stable political regime

It is absolutely essential (for any online enterprise) that there is not a political seesaw in the place where your company is based. Many countries (certainly the UK and the US) have so little real differences between the main parties that elections have become triumphs of spin over substance. This is very good for business as violent swings in taxation and policy make investing in anything as uncertain as online too risky to contemplate.

However, some tax havens still offer a real political gap between the main parties and it is important that today's online investment policy doesn't become tomorrow's piece of ideological nonsense.

Of all the online domiciles studied, the Channel Islands are ideal in many ways, as they offer enough infrastructure to be viable and no political disagreements whatsoever.

Security of data and transmission

Online entrepreneurs and investors, wherever they locate their businesses, are very concerned that they won't be forced to disclose data on individuals without good cause. This is essential in any business, as security of customer data and details is something which you must be able to promise before customers will sign up with you.

When Tony Blair proposed that internet service providers in the UK would have to disclose the details of any e-mails and web data they carried to government (and bear the cost of doing so), he become responsible for one of the biggest shifts of investment out of the UK in its history. Irish development officials said they had to get disillusioned US investors to form a queue as they pulled plans for creating online companies in Britain. Investors simply will not tolerate obligations to disclose and in the fickle online world they can move anywhere to avoid it. One and only one thing about online remains constant – its ability to speed ahead of European legislators and policy makers.

CHECKPOINTS

- Check whether your online business could be run sensibly from a low tax jurisdiction.

- Check the lowest amount of tax you might suffer and whether you could obtain the status of an international trading company.

- Check that the jurisdiction you are considering has:

  - Affordable bandwidth

  - Skilled technicians and affordable hosting

  - A stable political regime

  - No obligation on businesses to disclose data without due legal process.

CHAPTER 11

The Team

The biggest myth peddled by large, traditional organizations since the war is that they could give you a job which would make you *matter*. It was partly to do with the noble ideal of getting the world economy back on its feet, mixed up with ideas about public service and building a better society.

And yet looking back over the last ten years these types of organization have been the most perfidious and unpleasant to work for. They have repaid the loyalty of their long-serving staff by sacking them or easing them out in the most unpleasant ways, arguing the need for 'leaner, fitter teams' or using that useful all-purpose word 'underperformance'.

This has resulted in a new generation of workers who prefer not to work for these old organizations. In fact, they despise the people who manage them, doubting whether they have created any wealth and accusing them of being on a gravy train powered by intrigue and office politics.

So when Professor Rosabeth Moss Kantor[1] came out with the phrase in the late 1980s, 'it's not whether you are employed but whether you are employable', it had a huge resonance. Add to that the rapid shift in the nature of the consumer in the late 1990s and an individual is born who, at work, is no longer looking for certainty and importance but for two seemingly contradictory ideas, financial gain and lifestyle.

They don't want to *matter* anymore. That is an illusion which captivated their parents. But it would be useful to become 'seriously rich' and then do whatever makes them feel good. It is all about getting exactly what they want at the point they want it. In the latter category can fall anything from teaching karate to being a non-executive director of a dot.com. But they don't want to matter, that is for politicians and media tycoons who are something to do with a bygone age.

All of this is important when building your online business because unless you understand what motivates the new worker you won't be able to recruit and keep them.

Nasty things to do to an online employee

Absolutely the worst kind of organization you can create for an online start-up is a hierarchy. This is a company where everyone is accountable to someone above them and, as long as they refer up and get permission on difficult decisions, everything (mainly their pension) will be all right. This, if it ever worked, only works in a very stable business environment where no one has to react to any serious outside threats. However the environment in the year 2001 is not like that, the world is governed by technological change and a hierarchical structure does not allow staff to react quickly enough to what is happening around them.

For example the early organograms for the BBC's new online services (in 1996) were extraordinary Christmas tree affairs culminating in an individual with more reporting lines going into him or her than Grand Central station.

The problem with this is that it only works if the boss really does know best and know everything. The organogram demands that bosses know everything that is going on further down the tree, so that they can report fully on progress to the people above them. In the BBC of that period this was made worse by not allowing subordinates to present to managers more than two steps above them in the tree.

Hierarchical tree structures produce an undesirable side effect that knowledge about what is going on is power. Keep enough information away from people further down the tree, about policy or even the outcome of meetings, and your power is assured. As you are the only person who fully knows what is going on, you are the only person who can control a project. And controlling successful projects brings a higher profile and more success.

However, this doesn't work for the organization as a whole. In a hierarchy in the online age, the workers know far more about online than the bosses. In a hierarchy this condition is a threat to the natural order of being.

What then happens is that middle management have great difficulty in controlling meetings or projects, as they simply don't understand enough about technology or the fast-changing business environment to make sensible presentations. Senior management becomes dissatisfied with their performance and, in return, middle management give their subordinates a hard time. Eventually their subordinates, realizing they don't have to put up with this and sensing they have a value on the external market, leave.

In the case of the BBC, dissatisfaction with the hierarchical structure resulted in one of the greatest mass exoduses in any media organization in the past decade. People either left in frustration or were forced to leave as they weren't supporting the natural order of being. It is a wonder that the BBC established any online presence at all (CCN Interactive had already beaten them by two years). Essentially the BBC was saved by the power of its media brand and not by the intelligence of its organization.

The lesson here is a simple one; the amount of specialist knowledge you need in order to build an online organization means that you can't impose a 'boss knows best' structure. It simply won't work. Unimpressed by your assertion that 'you know best', your workers will leave.

Many European organizations still try to run online using this kind of structure. However, this old-fashioned approach will show in your staff turnover. The staff retention rate needs close monitoring and, if it exceeds a staff turnover of 20% a year in your online division, the structure will require urgent examination.

California

Silicon Valley in California became aware of this problem early on. The roots of the Valley lie in the 1930s oil boom and the oil companies had always been great experimenters with company structures. There is an old joke that a circuit board and the organogram of an oil company are basically the same.

But by the early 1990s Silicon Valley had a very pressing problem. Technological change was happening so quickly that if an executive was offered a slice of a patent in the morning, had he not taken it, by the afternoon it would have gone to a competitor. There was no point in referring up. By the time it got far enough 'up' for a decision a week would have elapsed.

Therefore, companies such as semiconductor manufacturer Intel decided to take a series of radical steps. The first was to completely trust its executives to act in the company's best interests. This is, unfortunately, a leap of faith which many European companies are reluctant to take even in the year 2001. To ensure that an executive's perception of the interests of the company and the company's real interests were coincident, Intel decided to codify the values by which an 'Intel person' should be guided. It created a set of ten values and for good measure printed them on the back of the company's security passes which hang around every employee's neck. This may seem extreme but Intel claims it works.

In addition Intel undertook the most extraordinary experiments with the company's structure, and created a 'matrix management', which meant that on any project a single individual could answer to two separate bosses in two separate departments. This had the advantage that a very junior employee and the president of the company could end up working together on the same project, which benefited the flow of ideas and the rate of innovation.

Intel also decided that the speed of technological change was so great that it was impossible for any single executive to keep an eye on strategic issues and do their daytime job. So it put two people into every executive job and called it 'two in a job'.

Now, before cynical European readers of this book laugh their heads off at the wacky world of Californian management, all this has a very serious point – how does a high technology organization survive (and thrive) in a period of unprecedented technological change? All online companies need to have an answer to this, because the entry barriers which the likes of, for example, lastminute.com have around its business model are very low indeed and a slight adjustment in the technological environment could get them into great trouble – and probably will, unless they are formidable business people.

Intel is an example of what is called the 'matrix' solution to the problem of team working in high tech industries. It is, in my opinion, unsuitable for new online businesses because it is wasteful. No one in a start-up can afford to employ two people in one job. The only reason Intel can is because it has always enjoyed spectacular growth and is now one of the richest companies in the world.

Sleepless in Seattle

The world's biggest software company, Microsoft, also has a solution to this problem. Despite Bill Gates' 'Silicon Bully' reputation, he has always been intelligent about how to get the best out of his staff. Early on, he used the power of the computer networks to structure his company. So in Microsoft there is an executive office, led by Gates, feeding out strategy to teams which come together simply for the duration of a project and get their lead and their feedback via computer networks. Gates' teams have to work this way as they are often so virtual that it is only computer networks which glue them together.

However, Gates has added an ingredient of his own – competition. Microsoft discovered, when it was rushing to finish its word processing package Word, that more is not better. It discovered that about 40 was the maximum number of people who could usefully work on a piece of software – 20 writing the code and 20 checking it for bugs. Double those numbers and more bugs went in with each rewrite than came out.

Gates got into the habit of creating *two* teams of 40 people to work on the same project but in direct competition with each other. One might come up with a more elegant solution than the other and also beat the deadline. At which point all the other team's work could be thrown away.

This is the competitive form of online organization. Again the boss stands back, having laid out the broad strategy, while self-governing teams get on with the work.

But it doesn't work in online start-ups because they can't afford to run teams in competition. However, the boss standing back, as Gates does, is an essential component of online team management.

Structure is not organization

Management guru Tom Peters said very early on in his career that 'structure is not organization'. In this cryptic comment lies the secret of how to build and motivate an online team.

What Peters meant was that drawing a chart of reporting lines in an organization rarely tells you how it works in practice. Consider, if you are in an organization, how you get things done. You network with friends, get initiatives going through working with others not in your reporting lines, and exchange information in the bar. These things are not shown in the company structure. So why do you do them?

The answer is because you are motivated, in some way, to take the initiative. It is said that in intelligent organizations it is better to seek forgiveness than permission; the argument being that if it goes wrong you can say sorry but at least you tried to get it done. One of the ways of discovering if you are in a hierarchy is to try this approach and if you get your knuckles rapped you are definitely in one!

The challenge in an online start-up is to produce an organization which is so flexible and intelligent that the structure does not matter. The way to do this is to concentrate on motivation, not on structure. The big consultancies are known to produce complex organograms for online start-ups which have fewer people than their own photocopying departments. They would be better thinking about what makes people want to come to work.

First it is worth thinking about the reasons why people *don't* join online start-ups. They are:

- Need for certainty

- Love of identity (a job which really matters)

- Need for a pension

- In-house training

- Annual bonus scheme

- Life insurance

- A large, personal office

- A top-of-the-range company car

- A large expense account

- The need to spend more time with one's family.

Although they may not admit it, most people want these things out of a job. You will not attract these people. In fact, you *must not* attract these people. Ultimately they will be bad for your business because they will be unnerved by it.

Shockers

There are two reasons most people join an online start-up. The more intangible one I will call 'shock'. The people who are driven by it are 'shockers'. It involves trying to do the following things:

- Create a new market

- Upset an old market

- Do business in a completely new way

- Be first in something new

- Shock old-fashioned companies

- Show someone else you were right.

Some people are highly motivated by this. They sometimes go as far as saying that they don't do it for the money (this is not entirely true).

However, you will have a larger number of these people than you think in any online organization, and they will work very hard for you if you give them a very loose structure and a lot of motivation.

How do you motivate people who are not primarily driven by money? Essentially the common theme is that they want to be seen to be different and to be proud of working for their online company.

The answer is to use promotion and publicity. These types of people want to change things so the thing to do is to convince them that is what they are doing. The most avid readers of any company's publicity are its own employees. Therefore, employing a public relations company for $15,000/month will be the best motivational investment you can make, particularly when it includes a portrait of you as a far-sighted and visionary online leader, the sort of person any shocker will follow to the ends of the earth.

Often a shocker will be someone with interesting ideas who has departed from (or been kicked out of) a big organization. They are not stuck for theories, and often have been involved in selling ideas, such as consultants, marketers or media.

It is true that the shockers don't work primarily for money but money helps to bind them in so it is as important to treat them in the same way as their more money-conscious colleagues.

However, they also have a shocking characteristic and one which can drag under your online venture – a tendency to perfection. Perfection is a dangerous idea in a small company as few companies, even large ones, have the resources to achieve it.

A software shocker will spend an enormous amount of time trying to get a piece of software engineered to the highest specifications, far higher than the market needs or appreciates. The trick with shockers is to keep telling them what is good for the company and get them to forget about what will impress their software writing friends.

Shockers and consultants are an expensive combination. Consultants have a vested interest in increasing their hold on the client. So they are constantly seeking to hold think sessions and away-days in order to dominate their client's thought processes and spending. Shockers love away-days because they can use it to argue for increased resources on things which they care about but the customers don't. Both types are excellent at coming up with compelling reasons for spending time on irrelevance. Therefore both need to be controlled carefully and kept apart. The trick in these businesses is to work the shockers hard in areas where they won't take over your business strategy. The same is true of consultants, use them for what you need them for but don't let them run the show. Either path leads to an excessive drain of time and cash on things that you don't need.

Owners

The second category of online employee is an 'owner'. Owners are there because they want a slice of the action and they believe that eventually the business will make them rich. Unless you do something really silly (such as insisting on your own bathroom), these people will stay very loyal to you while the business is matching its business plan.

Owners are easy to motivate, you give them a salary and a slice of the equity. It is best to give them equity, as it allows you to be meaner with cash in the start-up phase. I know of online businesses where people have been on $15,000/year in the early phases but with 2% of the equity. This really improves a business's cash flow.

Judging how much equity to give out to employees is important as eventually each will find out what the other has. One method of apportioning equity is the earlier you join the more you get, as in the beginning you were taking a bigger risk. A generous stake is 2%. The business plan, however unrealistic it is, can be used to demonstrate how well off the employees will be in five years. Everyone has a dream of buying a yacht or paying off a mortgage, so exploit this human fallibility.

Ownership, however small, is a way to bring the shockers into line. A shocker with a stake will be bound by peer group pressure when it comes to implementing decisions about how resources should be used. It is important to get everyone to understand that you are leaving certain features off the new version of the software which you are about to release because then you can afford to meet the business plan targets (and, by implication, you will all get rich). Some individuals may disagree but it will be too difficult for them to dissuade their colleagues, all of whom have a stake in the success of the business.

All of this allows you to run the business. But how do you choose your owners and shockers – how do you build a team which will work together?

Typecasting

Online businesses rely on project teams. Project teams are the strongest and simplest way of building an online business, as they:

- Allow problems to be tackled by the best people for that job quickly and flexibly

- Make it hard for a hierarchical structure to emerge which, if it develops, will make your expensive and valuable recruits leave.

A team is an interesting business phenomenon as it is small and relies on cooperation between its members to achieve its goals. Online start-ups typically begin as a single small team and then acquire and train other employees who can work in a similar way. This is the reason that people recruited to dot.coms from corporations often fail to make the grade as they are not used to teamwork and the strange mixture of assertion and compromise implicit in it.

Assertion

Teamworkers have to be able to compromise in order to live with the shared aims of a team because:

- They have their private doubts about the way the majority of the team wishes to undertake the strategy
- Their personal agenda does not coincide with the shared aims of the group.

Most people from corporations are used to this. However, they are not used to *asserting their creativity*. This is what makes teams work better than hierarchies at finding quick and flexible solutions to problems. Assertion is necessary to make teams work and is the skill most lacking from long-term big company employees. They are used to:

- Aggression – being downright unpleasant in order to get their own way
- Politics – doing someone else down in order to weaken them
- Self-publicity – getting things done by raising their profile and your power.

These methods are fine in large organizations where the contracts keep coming in and someone has to organize them but in a team running a start-up they are almost useless. In order for a team to work, individuals need to say what they think and influence others with their knowledge without annoying them. This is assertion.

Most large company people are bad at this, although it does depend on how long they have been with a corporation and whether they feel the company does things in a reasonable way.

Therefore, it is essential to understand the attitude of anyone who is leaving a large organization to join an online one. Are they able to assert their views reasonably and in a convincing and polite manner?

Abilene

It is easy to create an ethos in which, despite everyone asserting them-selves, teams all end up sharing the same mindset. Online businesses notably are prone to this because the founders tend to share a rosy view about the business and have had to fight a lot of doubters to get it off the ground. The doubters were wrong and they were right. That is why they have come together. This leaves the management team wonderfully united but also prone to shared delusions.

It is known as 'the abilene principle',[2] the phenomenon where a group of people come to a conclusion that no sane individual left to their own devices would ever endorse. The executives of political parties are extremely prone to it.

This condition is extremely dangerous for online teams because:

- Abilene groups think themselves invulnerable and take extraordinary risks, which no sane individual manager would take

- Abilene groups are very adept at finding reasons to explain away evidence that does not fit their business view (such as bad sets of finan-cial results)

- Abilene groups think their competitors are stupid or without merit. They fail to see them as serious threats.

Abilene thinking means that your company has lost its grasp on reality and is basing its strategy on delusion. If it is drifting further and further from its business plan and explanations of underperformance are becoming less not more comprehensible, then it is possible that the team needs recon-necting with reality.

Essential to this is an outsider on the management team who is capable of making insiders see the company and its environment in a different way. If the progress of the business is simply a question of timing (being ahead of the market), then the team has to see that it might take the market some time to catch up.

In order to avoid the Abilene principle and also the danger of the team degenerating into a series of fights where old-style corporate politics takes over, it is important that there are various contrasting types of person at the top of an online company.

Picking the right stuff

There is a lot of literature on how to get the right mixture of personality types. Some of the most interesting thinking came from management thinker and writer R.M. Belbin.

Belbin conducted a lot of research into team composition which upheld what everyone intuitively knows about business – that if you put the brightest people together in a room they don't come up with the best results. Belbin discovered that a mix of different types of people worked best together. Unfortunately, he then went on to make the mistake of trying to define these types and to give them strange names. Belbin's types have now achieved cult status with some consultants, rivalling the passion with which tabloid readers adhere to signs of the zodiac. Sometimes they appear to be useful, but more often they are so vague as to be completely useless. For the record the types are:

- *The chairman* – presides over the team and coordinates its efforts

- *The shaper* – passionate and driven and pushes for the task to get done

- *The plant* – the source of original ideas and proposals

- *The monitor-evaluator* – the analyst. Necessary as a quality check

- *The resource-investigator* – the popular one who brings new contacts, ideas and developments

- *The company worker* – the practical organizer who turns ideas into manageable tasks

- *The team worker* – holds the team together by listening and being supportive

- *The finisher* – the one who follows through and makes sure the team is meeting its deadlines.[3]

This is all very well but most small organizations cannot afford to employ all these people simply in order to have perfectly balanced teams. A selection criteria for staff concentrating on these psychological attributes is unrealistic, particularly for an online start-up.

One of the results of Belbin's findings is that people often present themselves to you as a Belbin type. It is normally men who are trying to sell consultancy who announce within two minutes of meeting you: 'I'm a plant.'

Belbin tries to analyse group variety in terms of personality. I believe that with online companies this is best done in terms of role. No organization can get by without using the attributes which Belbin describes; however, in most organizations, one person at different times plays more than one of these roles.

The five most useful *responsibilities* in an online organization are:

- *Chairman* – chairs meetings and creates a consensus if there isn't one. Helps with contacts and networks (Belbin's 'resource-investigator'). Most importantly, someone who brings external reality to tightly cohesive teams so preventing the team going Abilene. This is a role which Belbin doesn't mention

- *Chief executive* – oversees company strategy, both financial and business, and drives it through using both people and resources

- *Finance director* – essential for keeping tabs on cash flow. Bad cash flow is the most common cause of online company collapse. Online businesses, in their early years, are best controlled through the cheque book as it keeps teams and staff disciplined with a simple benchmark which everyone can understand. Market share and other metrics are too far removed from the cash flow issue to be useful. The finance director is also responsible for raising new funds. Most online companies need refinancing at some point

- *Sales director* – concentrates on defining and selling the products of the business. Unless your company is bringing in revenue it won't survive

- *Marketing director* (or manager) – coordinates the positioning and promotion of the company. New companies need to make consumers aware of their presence and establish a brand.

There are online companies who set up with a plethora of roles, including customer relationship director and information technology director. However, this can lead to a lack of focus. If a business is to move fast and effectively, it needs concentrated and fast decision-making so that implementation can be left to project teams.

How do you find these people? This is not easy, but the best recruitment method is to find the young who have not been given enough headroom in bigger organizations (but have not yet been corrupted by 'big organization think').

Headhunters can be employed, although they are rather expensive. The best method is to retain someone on contract whose job is to look after recruitment and who has a large network in the area in which you are trading. Networks and personal recommendation are the most powerful tools when looking for good staff. It will be helpful to tap into as many personal networks as possible.

People are the single most important resource an online company possesses. They determine whether you can change your business if conditions change, which in the online environment they often do. Don't squander your people by treating them as if they were working for a corporation. They probably joined you to escape one.

CHECKPOINTS

■ The modern consumer has changed and so has the modern employee. Employees tend to want to have responsibility, the opportunity to become wealthy and achieve a lifestyle which makes them happy. They do not want to define themselves through a job title, which is now considered old fashioned.

■ Never organize an online operation as a hierarchy.

■ If more than 20% of your staff are leaving a year, check whether it is because you have unwittingly created a hierarchy.

■ Many people like and enjoy working for corporations. However they make bad online employees. Make sure you don't recruit them.

■ Online employees tend to come in two varieties:

   ■ Shockers – who want to change the world

   ■ Owners – who are prepared to take risks in order to make themselves wealthy.

■ Both shockers and owners need careful handling but both should be bound into group decisions by some degree of ownership of the company.

■ Organize online companies as autonomous teams, with strategy being set by a chief executive.

■ Guard against your management team developing the same mindset – of going 'Abilene'. This means they will ignore reality and make very strange decisions. The best antidote is an independent chairman.

- Recruit people who can fulfil five essential roles. Do not worry about psychological personality types, they are for big companies. The five roles are:

  - Chairman

  - Chief executive

  - Finance director

  - Sales director

  - Marketing director.

CHAPTER 12

How to Use It All

The spring of 2000 was the peak of the online boom. By the autumn of 2000, there were many well-publicized failures. By the end of 2000, $1 billion of online investment was disappearing every month.

Why has this happened? Basically because the rules of normal company start-ups apply equally well to online, despite a belief by early investors that somehow new economy companies would produce a step change so that *unless* you were online you would fail. But like all start-ups, it appears that 80% of online companies fail in their first two years. What we are seeing at the beginning of 2001 is the shake-out.

Nasty name, nasty business

FuckedCompany.com is a nasty site – although a very famous and popular one in the US and the UK. It doesn't merely relay rumours about internet companies heading for the rocks, it revels in them. For example:

'Rumor has it CarStation.com is letting 75% of their remaining staff go, one-by-one. The objective, to close the entire SF office by next month.' (12/26/00)

'Rumor has it provider of 'consumer health information', HeathScout.com, laid off around 50%. Another $100 million down the drain … swish swish.' (12/22/2000)

'Rumor has it BizBuyer.com just laid off 90% of their staff (170 people?) and shut down.' (12/20/2000)

'Universal's highly polished venture into the world of online pay-me-for-access-to-bandwidth-robbing-slow-loading-chunky-ass-videos-that-give-me-a-headache, FarmClub.com, served 40% of its employees pithy pink crumpets with their morning coffee.' (12/20/2000)

The site demonstrates a visceral loathing for venture capitalists and really anyone who has made a less than successful investment in an online start-up. Much of it consists

---

simply of abuse. Also, and unforgivably, it trades rumours, which means you are likely to be worried by seeing your company there when the information is merely gossip. But so inextricably linked is the internet to the US right to free speech that all US sites ought to carry a health warning.

However, the site does reflect the chaos involved in online investment at the end of the year 2000.

Old economy companies have lost their fear of online, seen the consumer demand for it and set up online enterprises of their own. This has seriously dented stand-alone online competitors. For example, a shoal of online start-ups had internet banking to themselves for the first year. First-e group plc, an internet bank in Britain and Germany, recently merged with Uno-e of Spain. It seems that it has already spent the best part of 200 million euros but is now unlikely to be worth anything like the $2.3 million it declared at the time. First-e's problem is that traditional banks have now started their own internet operations and have matched the mouth-watering savings rates which online banks used to attract early customers. In the end it seems that consumers prefer traditional 'bricks and clicks' to clicks alone. Traditional banks have invested billions over the years in building up trust in their brand. Online companies are now feeling the cold comfort of competing directly against these trusted brands with little technological advantage.

There is also a subtler problem shared by many of the dot.com start-ups. Big traditional companies have built up a discipline of running a business, something that many online start-ups are trying to learn as they go along. Sometimes the process of making a decision in a large company will hand an advantage to the fast-moving start-up, but in a long battle with a traditional customer base (as in banking), the sheer discipline of the machine you are up against will begin to tell. One of the classic texts on business strategy puts this in a nutshell:

A highly formalized system of planning is no guarantee of success but, equally, leaving things to chance constitutes the best guarantee of failure. The key to success is not so much in the adoption of a formal approach to strategy formulation but rather in the *quality and consistency* of the implementation and in the organization's ability to adapt to an ever changing business environment.[1]

In other words online start-ups leave too much to chance and don't have the quality and consistency of large traditional companies.

Essentially this is what this book is about. I hope that it gives you the courage to think seriously about your online ideas and also a discipline and framework in which to implement them so that you won't be at a disadvantage when a large, well-organized company counterattacks. If you are successful, they will do just that.

Use the checkpoints in this book

In order to avoid the disasters that befell Boo.com, Breathe.com, PetsPyjamas, Netimperative or even Clickmango, use the checkpoints laid out in the chapters so far to make sure that your online idea has wings and should fly. Too many online start-ups fail because there is a fault in the initial analysis of their business prospects. All the chapters up to now have been designed to scan your online proposition for faults. It is never worth raising others' money, purchasing a boat, and setting to sea in a leaking vessel. The payback, if it comes at all, will be too short. You might as well have stuck to the daytime job.

Taking each of the chapters in turn, you will be able to tick off what your online idea should deliver if it has a chance of success.

The quicksilver consumer

Does your idea actually appeal to the new consumer who appeared suddenly at the end of the 20th century? This consumer has money but little time and so time is very precious to them.

The most obvious example of a device which exactly serves this type of consumer is the electronic programme guide, which enables a viewer to see on their TV screen what is being transmitted on the 300 or so digital channels on SkyDigital for up to two and a half days in advance. It correctly assumes that people no longer have the time or the inclination to search through listings magazines for a programme they want to watch. They want *exactly what they want when they want it.*

Examples of the kind of things which will fail this consumer are inefficient home delivery services (as Toys R Us and Urban Fetch discovered) and search facilities which are dense and incomprehensible – anything in fact which fails to deliver exactly what this consumer wants in time and to order. They are very unforgiving and won't try you again, something from which your carefully constructed brand will not recover.

Supply chain reactions

Are you attacking the supply chain at the point at which you can be most powerful? It is pointless setting up as an internet service provider providing internet access to the customer when you own some of the most powerful content on the internet (as Virgin.com discovered). Use your assets to give you a powerful position in your supply chain so that others come to you.

The technology test

Is your idea really an online idea? Many online start-ups have had to retreat into becoming home delivery operations served by paper catalogues because there simply wasn't the demand online for their idea.

This is true of the pets market. Online entrepreneurs got very excited about the pets market in 1999, which accounted for $3 billion of sales in the US alone. They concluded that pet owners would flock online. They were wrong.

Detailed market research, done after a plethora of pet sites had launched, concluded that owners thought of pets not as pets but as members of their family and so shopped for them when they shopped for the rest of the family – which was at the supermarket. Also the broad spectrum of pet owners simply were not drawn from the new consumers. They had the time to amble around supermarkets with the dog tethered outside the store (something which is hard to imagine the new consumer has time to do).

One always knows that an online enterprise is in trouble when they take refuge in other forms of distribution. Take Charles Fallon, chief executive of Pets Pyjamas who said: 'It is very hard for an internet business to make money solely as an internet business. More and more dot.coms are introducing traditional catalogue businesses as part of their propositions.'

In December 2000 Pets Pyjamas went bust. As Campaign commented: 'To be honest it's a wonder these guys ever thought it would work in the first place.'[2] However, it could have worked had the proposition been one which should have been online. Pets Pyjamas might have done better had they spent the money on a lavish marketing campaign aimed at catalogue shoppers and then created the world's best home delivery service, with no need for technology at all.

However, there are a number of people who want to be online pet retailers, including Petopia, Petsmart, Petz.co.uk and Petplanet. It may well turn out that they are all barking up the wrong tree.

Timing

This is one of the most difficult and important tests your online idea must pass. Being too far ahead of the market, or the technology, could mean years of losses and often that the business is not viable.

One of the commonest reasons for thinking there is a market when there isn't is to get the demographics of the internet wrong. Although it is estimated that, in the UK, almost 50% of the population have access (at work or in the home) to the internet, that demographic is heavily skewed to higher earners and income groups. For example, the *Sun* newspaper set up its 'Currant Bun' website – and promoted it heavily in its newspaper – but, given the demographics of the web, it was always unlikely that the *Sun*'s downmarket readership would use it. They didn't, and it closed towards the end of 2000.

Despite all the website disasters in 2000, it is interesting to note that no gardening website has failed to date. This is counterintuitive as you would expect gardeners to be technophobes. But they are in the higher, more affluent demographic which is beginning to find the web useful.

Clearly some markets thrive online and others are yet to be born. Careful research is therefore needed into any target market before investing money.

Even trickier are the new technologies, which may exist but are not yet affordable enough to use as part of a viable business. A prime example of this is Breathe.com, run (and partly owned) by a successful telecoms entrepreneur, Martin Dawes. He had decided that the time was right to offer free internet access, coupled with unmetered telephone charges, for a one-off lifetime fee of £50. His business model would have made money through advertising and a commission on sales through the site.

However, unmetered telephone access is still not available in the UK at an economic rate to telephone time resellers such as Breathe, and Breathe breathed its last in December 2000, although PricewaterhouseCoopers is trying to find a buyer.

A simple analysis would have showed that the numbers in the plan weren't viable and if Dawes was betting that telephone access would rapidly liberalize in the UK, it would have been a triumph of hope over experience. One investor subsequently admitted that unmetered access for a monthly fee would have been viable and the figures showed that.

Although market timing and technology seem hard to judge, an in-depth examination of the existing information will tell you if there is a market or affordable technology for your product. Many of the first wave of online entrepreneurs wilfully ignored this information.

Defining the market

If your idea has passed the first four tests, it is worth thinking about how you will position it so that it can easily move to market domination. Go for a market which clearly exists in the imagination of your target customers but which is not being served properly by the existing players.

Some examples:

- California-based Napster defined a market for free downloading of pop music over the internet. It captured 38 million users in a year. It is now trying to convert this model to a subscription service with the support of German media giant Bertlesmann.

- DomainAudit in the UK spotted that there may be a lot of domain registration companies, but few managed and protected the domains. It has now moved to a position of market leadership in Europe in this newly defined market.

Amazon.com, foreseeing the online book market before anyone else did, continues to grow as a result of its market dominance. In November 2000, for example, it was the first UK site to pass a million users a month, attracting 1.2 million visitors – up from 865,000 in October. As a market leader, it can change the market it operates in by innovating in it.

So it has filed a patent for its 'Associates Programme', a piece of software which keeps track of book recommendations from other websites. In essence the idea is simple: if a site signs up for the programme it can promote a book on its website and provide a link to Amazon from which users can buy the book. If they do buy, the Amazon software keeps a record of where the reference comes from and pays commission to the referring site. Essentially, Amazon is exploiting its pre-eminence in the book market to move into e-commerce applications. Last year this invention created more than $1 billion in sales in e-commerce markets worldwide.

Defining a market correctly leads to dominance and the ability to create barriers and inventions with which the competition simply can't keep pace.

Online branding

Branding will make your online enterprise so compelling that users will form a psychological bond with it. In the online world it is possible to use a whole array of electronic branding devices which were not possible before the advent of computer technology. However, it is amazing how few entrepreneurs exploit the powerful technologies on which their enterprise is based in order to create a brand.

Think about this carefully, as it could mean that you are the only memorable online enterprise in your market. In the pet supply market it could have been decisive.

Planning the pitch

It is all very well having a watertight online idea – but can you sell it? Most good ideas fail to get funding due to lack of presentation skills. Even the best management team in the world can let you down in this way – as many people are scared of presenting to an audience.

Also you need to make sure that your plan highlights the areas which investors know are peculiar to online companies and which you will have to get right.

In the end careful planning of how to exploit the psychology of the presentation will make your team attractive even in the eyes of stuffy merchant bakers and accountants. Investors are only human after all – exploit the fact.

Doing the numbers

There are also certain numbers which investors will want to see. Pitching them correctly is a matter of judging what looks good without looking incredible. Unfortunately all the business plans I have ever seen inflate revenues and profits; sometimes unintentionally, sometimes not. Yours will have to do the same to stand comparison with other plans against which you will be competing.

Partnerships

A partnership is ideal if it adds something which your online business lacks; which may be as simple as cash. However the best way to make your online proposal fly is to find a partner who not only invests in your business but also has skills or contacts which your business lacks.

Use the method in this chapter to work out what your business lacks and then spend some time finding a backer who can give you these skills, either through managing or commissioning them or because they have them already. If you are already funded give useful partners an equity share in your business so that you don't have to pay out cash for their services in the early cash-poor stages of your business.

The where

It is extraordinary how few entrepreneurs consider where they are going to locate their online business at their inception. Online businesses are virtual so it doesn't matter where they are located as they can generally be accessed inexpensively from anywhere in the world. The offshore online betting companies which have appeared in centres such as the Channel Islands, Malta and Gibraltar are shining examples of how unfair taxes can be avoided by relocating an online enterprise. When corporation tax rates of 20% are routinely available outside the UK why should the online entrepreneur pay more? Always consider the location of your business – particularly as part of your presentation to investors. The tax rates available to online entrepreneurs should make their mouths water.

The team

Teams are difficult – so it is important to spend some time getting them right. People are employed in online mainly for their skills and ideas so they need careful handling, otherwise their ideas and skills will dry up or, worse, they will move elsewhere.

It is important to consider the structure of your business. Don't be like many large corporations who consider that everyone should have permission from three separate departments before making a change in online. Online changes all the time so successful teams must enjoy a high degree of trust and headroom in order to beat the competition.

Also do not fall into the classic online start-up trap where your board starts making stupid decisions because everyone on it has a common mindset. How the Breathe.com board agreed to keep trading when its business plan numbers didn't make sense from the start is bizarre. But it is probably because the board had collectively suspended reality (by agreement). Stay alert for this dangerous condition.

Now keep your online business trading successfully

The last section of this book deals with what to keep your eye on once you have launched your online business. Once launched, you have to keep a weather eye on the four basic elements that can go wrong most easily.

These are best thought of as the base of a pyramid. The analogy is that unless you have a firm base you cannot build an online brand.

The four elements you have to keep checking are:

Product check
Is your product relevant to the market you are targeting? Does that market find that your product (or products) gives them benefits they cannot get elsewhere from a conventional offline service? For example, people often use Ask Jeeves.com as it allows them to use seven search engines simultaneously on the internet. This, for a broad search, is clearly superior to Yahoo! (although Yahoo! has advantages of its own). Neither Yahoo! nor Ask Jeeves can be reproduced as conventional offline services.

Checking that the product is right is the most important base on the pyramid and essentially drives the way in which success or failure is determined by the other bases. As it is the primary driver of the pyramid base Chapter 13 is entirely devoted to product checking.

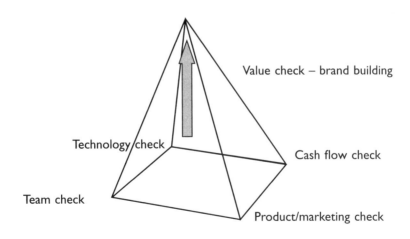

Figure 12.1 Factors to check in an online business

Technology check

Intimately wrapped up with the product check is the technology check. Does the technology you have commissioned support the product set which is best for your market?

This is no mean achievement. Most online businesses with which I have been closely involved have realised at some point that their target market in fact wants something different from what they originally planned. This involves rebuilding the software. It is therefore a mistake in business plans to leave a one-off lump sum for software development when software will constantly need to be redeveloped if you are tracking and following your market's needs. Don't be fooled by the lack of change in the appearance of Amazon – their software engineers are constantly refining and updating the software at the back end (which supports the screens the user sees). This allows them to track buying patterns more efficiently, track where buyers first see a book advertised on the net and even allow one click purchasing (a huge breakthrough in its own right).

Cash flow check

Cash flow in any start-up business is king – and online start-ups are no exception. However in online businesses I find that I have to redraft the cashflow plan once a month as revenue starts to come through from unexpected sources. This is particularly true in B2B enterprises where clients come along and demand an unexpected variation on your product offering. They may demand a huge volume of one particular product – in which case that product is going to have to be discounted for that client.

That is if the business is going well. If it is not, you need to be able to work out quickly how long the business can survive on the cash you have raised, and when it will need its next cash injection. Such calculations are vital as investors hate to receive sudden and unexpected demands for money. Always keep investors well informed – giving them monthly cash flow headlines is, with a start-up, the best way to do this.

Team check

The team check is the subtlest and most difficult thing to watch. Is the team performing individually and collectively? If there is a lot of friction, is it creative – or just producing heat?

Online start-ups are stressful places as they are typically testing an untried product with a team that has never worked together before. This is an area where existing traditional businesses have a big advantage as they can put together teams who are used to a certain way of working, and for whom, personally, the risk is lower.

If there are weaknesses in a team it is very easy to fire the wrong person. The difficulty may arise from a combination of factors; the most typical being lack of experience and a protracted decision-making process. If the team is not working together it is always best to convene and discuss it with a neutral party (someone who is not involved in the day-to-day running of the business). There is no point in listening to the complaints of individuals against others as they will not have an overall picture and will simply be relaying malicious gossip. Most problems are not personal – they are nearly always organisational.

This is why in start-ups the role of the chairman (or woman) is so important – as a neutral party who takes an overview of the business without being directly involved, but has the influence to solve team issues.

Value checking and brand building

The chapter on branding went into detail about the values and attributes it is necessary to give a brand so that consumers feel they have a tangible relationship with it. For example washing powders often build on values such as 'caring' and 'motherly' so that they can create the impression that if you use this soap powder you are caring for your children and family.

In order to build up an online brand it is essential to establish the values of that brand at inception and to use those values in its promotion. Don't be diverted by the team or the engineers who built the software and what the product means to them. The ultimate service is probably not aimed at their type of person!

The most important skill in managing an online company is to keep the base factors (at the bottom of the pyramid) all working while pushing heavily the values of the product and so building the brand. Of course if one of the base factors is wobbly it will weaken your attempts at brand building as you will be undermining the trust between your product and the consumer. Brand creation cannot occur in these circumstances. Ask Boo.com or Toys R Us, who found delivering on time to their online customers too difficult.

The pyramid implies that the whole purpose of getting your products, your technology, your team and your cashflow right is in order to build a brand. This is absolutely correct. Products come and go, but brands, once established, add a large goodwill margin to your profits. They also give you permission to enter other markets (in the way in which Virgin has moved from records to airlines, investments and trains).

Ultimately the task of the online entrepreneur is the same as that of the offline entrepreneur; to create profit and growth through establishing a strong brand.

CHECKPOINTS

- Big organisations may be slow but they often have superior planning and implementation skills compared to online start-ups. Make sure your start-up develops these skills by running through the following checks:

    - Does your online business idea appeal to the quicksilver consumer?

    - Are you attacking the supply chain at the correct point?

    - Is your idea really an online idea?

    - Is there a market for your product?

    - Is there the technology to support it?

    - Define your market so that you dominate it.

    - Exploit computer technology to create a powerful online brand.

    - Plan your business pitch so that investors will find it compelling.

    - Make sure your business plan includes the right numbers presented in the right way.

    - Find a partner who not only invests but also brings skills or contacts to your business.

    - Make sure your team contains the correct skills.

- When you are up and running constantly check the most important four elements of your online business:

    - That its product is relevant to the market it is serving.

    - That the technology supports the products the business is selling.

    - That cash flow is positive and that all potential sources of revenue are being exploited.

    - That your team is performing effectively.

    - That the values of your business are constantly being built on, enhanced and promoted in order to build up your brand.

CHAPTER 13

Product Checks

The most important check is the product check. Products define the relationship with the consumer in any business. If they are of variable quality, you have to spend more money, time and effort explaining the benefits of what you are selling.

In other words, it helps if your products are good and relevant and your customers know that they are good and relevant. However, given the history of software development, where consumers have come to tolerate a number of hiccups, ticks or bugs, many online businesses seem tempted to launch with products which are not properly tested and certainly not thought through.

There are three reasons that online products are not 'good' in the eye of the consumer:

- First, utility: in other words, your product fails to meet the demands of your customers. If your target customers find your product inappropriate, too difficult to understand, or less flexible than the competition they will gradually stop using it, however much money you have invested in its promotion. Understanding the usefulness of your product is done by *finding out* if it is useful. Market research used to be a long, expensive and tedious business, but computer technology now lets you research how your customers are using products from minute to minute. Many companies setting up online operations fail to incorporate online research tools into their technology and so lose the opportunity to refine products using instant market feedback.

- Second, customers are simply not aware of your product or its benefits. This is the main neurosis of the online entrepreneur, that their product is there on the shelves but possesses the profile of a submarine. Most online businesses have a sufficient grasp of communication to hire a public relations agency to launch their product, but this is a one-dimensional approach to getting an online product known.

■ Third, the product or business is insufficiently branded. Chapter 6 looked at the theory of brands and branding for online businesses. However, the branding of businesses should be seamlessly supported by the way in which the business deals with its customers. Online technology offers many new ways of doing this, which technology-based businesses often fail to use.

Utility – check that your product is delivering the goods

Everyone makes assumptions about what people want, even experienced entrepreneurs who should know better.

It is best summed up in the 'cake test'. Place two different cakes on a plate and ask two people which one they want. Eighty per cent of the time each will choose the one they *don't* want on the assumption that the other person really wants the one they do. Politeness makes you assume that they want what you want. However, people have different needs and tastes and in the cake test it is probably better to be selfish in order to fulfil the other person's real desires. They are more likely to have different tastes from you and want the other cake.

This is also true in business. People tend to assume that what they like is what everyone else will want and like. If the target group is 'people like you', then this is a good strategy as you can use yourself and your friends as a test (or focus) group. However, this is rarely the case.

The most common online product problem is that the engineers have rushed to build a piece of software to specification and, in doing so, have created something that only they like and understand. The rush to market means that there hasn't been time (or possibly money) to design the product around the needs and habits of the target customer.

So the views of the engineers tend to prevail. An example of this was a successful UK microcomputer of the mid-1980s, called the BBC micro, which after it was booted up presented the user with a screen which said: 'BBC BASIC>' … and then a huge expanse of empty greenness. Many years later a generation familiar with DOS and a command prompt might have an inkling (however small) about what to do next. However, the engineers had made no concessions to anyone buying that machine, you had to know about Basic to proceed. In fact, the packaging around the computer should have said 'do not buy this before you acquire a working knowledge of BASIC', but no such wording appeared.

Many successful software products still bear the hallmarks of their origins at the hands of the engineers. There is still, even on Word, a plethora of buttons and pull-down commands of which only 20% are ever used by most writers. Microsoft believes that to be the best the product has to have the most features, but this is solely an engineering obsession. The most successful domestic appliances often have the least buttons, the fridge, freezer or toaster. The car became more successful as it got simpler, it could be driven using a limited set of controls and didn't need someone with a mechanical mind to set things such as the air and gas mixture necessary on cars in the 1920s but later mechanized.

The first important product check, once you have launched, is 'can the user get up and running on my product quickly and easily?' Apple Computers ran a series of adverts showing a Dad who had bought a PC for his children for Christmas laboriously working through the instructions and failing to get it to work. Apple, being a closed system, is easier to assemble (although less well supplied with as wide a range of peripherals and software as PCs).

Let us compare two financial information sites, www.advfn.com and www.iii.co.uk. Interactive Investor International (iii.co.uk) is the elder of the two and has had longer to react to the way in which consumers use the site, and it shows. It is very difficult, looking at advfn.com, to work out what the 20 or so tabs at the top of its menu bar are for, whereas iii.co.uk's features are driven by the context of the page you are on – hence there are fewer buttons and all are directly relevant to what you are currently viewing. This makes it easier for the user to go to what they need to see when they want to see it. The modern web user, being time poor, normally demands that.

There are three ways to test how relevant pages and products are to the target audience:

- Test the product on a focus group

- Monitor page and customer use

- License the product.

Focus groups

Focus groups, which have had a bad press recently because of political parties using them as a substitute for political values, are still a powerful way of researching and refining products. In an ideal world, all online products and software would be tested in this way. The reality is that they

aren't. The scramble to get a product onto the market quickly and the difficulties of getting launch products working as specified, mean that there is
little time to test them on consumers until they are actually live on air and
failing to generate revenue.

Testing online ideas is difficult and expensive. Before a focus group can
comment on an online product they have to understand it and to do that
they have to see it working. It is no good describing the idea in the
abstract, as many online start-ups want to do, because online ideas are
often unfamiliar. It is always best to show focus groups a working demo,
as they might well point out blinding truths which an expensive management consultant could fail to uncover.

For example, research was conducted for a national newspaper into the
viability of a new business television channel. Different focus groups were
created, representing men and women of different ages.[1] They all said that
the last thing they wanted was another business television channel, even
from so distinguished a business news provider.

It was decided to explore an interactive business channel. Interactive TV
is text, figures, even clips of video on demand delivered via the television
and already exists in the UK on platforms such as SkyDigital's. It was a
long shot as research to date showed that the focus groups were so conservative that they would not use any kind of television for their business news.

Naturally the focus groups had never seen interactive TV, so a demonstration was created for them. Surprisingly, they loved it.

The reason was that they hated the way conventional TV forced them to
see a lot of material which was irrelevant. These were busy people who
found that conventional business television wasted their time. But a
medium which allowed them to select material, from their television, at a
time of their choosing, fitted their needs and lifestyle. These were interesting findings as, at the time, many experts predicted that interactive TV
offered little advantage over its conventional predecessor and would not
be adopted by any television users with any enthusiasm.

The advantage of focus group research is that it gives a qualitative reaction to a product. It gives intuition, emotion and quotes, and thus the business will have an idea of how the product will be received when it is up
and running in the market.

Monitor customer use

Computer technology provides online businesses with an enormous, ability
to monitor customers and their spending habits. However, it is remarkable

how few new online operations build this into their marketing planning. In fact, an online business can have its quantitative product checking designed into its software from launch. This section gives some examples of effective automated product checking.

The simplest form of customer monitoring is recording the use of a site, or specific pages on a site, using software. These data allow the entrepreneur to see when the site is being accessed (Figure 13.1). This can contain some useful indicators. For example, three years ago Interactive Bureau, a graphic design company in New York, discovered that it not only had a peak of visitors to its site at lunchtime but also another peak at 3 am in the morning. Lunchtime was easy to explain – employees could look at what they wanted using their employer's internet access. The 3 am peak indicated the strong following that the site had in Europe, where the time was 9 am European time.

This kind of software can also be used to monitor the use of individual pages. However, the days of a permanent page on a website are long gone. Many web pages are created now as one-offs from several elements in a database in response to a unique request by a visitor for content or information. That page will probably only exist for as long as the user

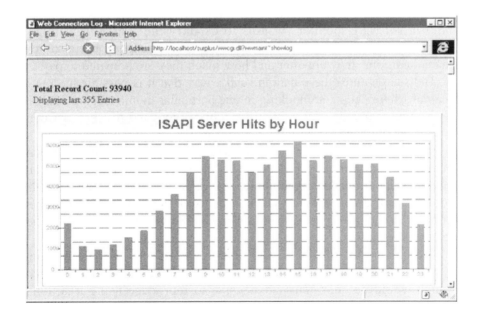

Figure 13.1 A page showing hits per hour from the Surplus 3 site

continues to ask that exact same question and with exactly that set of information stored in the database of the site.

So online content is ever changing and so is the customer information which can be extracted from it. Most 'visitor behaviour' software now looks at several pieces of data and brings them together. For example, Microsoft's Visual FoxPro web software is capable of looking at the number of hits a site gets from different sources. So, for example, if a visitor arrives from another site (such as Yahoo!), the software will monitor what they request and also how much they spend (if it is an e-commerce site).

Pulling this information together can give the online entrepreneur an idea of where visitors arrive from, what they ask for and how much they spend when they get there. This allows the entrepreneur not only to monitor the popularity of his products but also to take a view of the sites which send him the highest spenders, allowing him to calculate the level he is prepared to pay these sites for a presence on them, either in the form of pages or banner advertising.

Some online operations want to know immediately about sales enquiries so that they can follow them up using traditional media such as the telephone. This gives entrepreneurs the ability to monitor product performance in real time.

A good example of this is the software which CD9.com has built for Countryside Properties, a traditional bricks and mortar housebuilder. The built-in software monitors visitors to Countryside's large website and monitors not only where visitors are looking for property but also how many bedrooms they are after and how much they are prepared to pay for it. The site captures these data in such a way that it is possible to draw a map of where people are looking in one particular month (Figure 13.2) or how popular an area of the country is with visitors and so whether Countryside should consider building houses there.

Most important, the site can alert Countryside to any particular kinds of enquiry which might be of interest to them. For example, if there are enquiries about four-bedroom houses over £400,000 in the south-west, the software will e-mail Countryside's sales team and Countryside can then pursue the enquiry by telephone (as long as the visitor has left his or her telephone details).

The importance of this kind of software cannot be overstated. Quite simply, it creates a continuous stream of information about customers which would be enormously expensive to reproduce using traditional market research methods. It initiates an age of business in which businesses will be expected to respond because they no longer have the excuse that they didn't realize early enough that their product was no good. Now

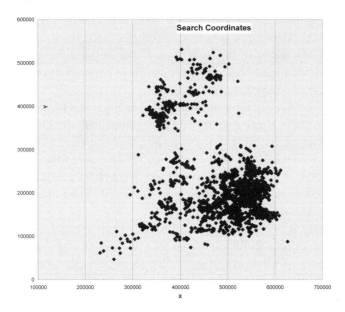

Figure 13.2 Enquiries about properties from the Countryside website over a month mapped by their coordinates

the evidence will be there instantly, giving them time to fight back with better and better products.

In digital television this kind of responsiveness is already available to operators running video on demand and pay per view services. Whatever programmes or films that viewers order is information which is immediately available to the broadcaster. It means that television will become more like a supermarket, in which customer habits can be seen from till receipts. At the moment television relies on crude mass audience figures (ratings) to gauge demand for their programming. No wonder so many viewers, whose viewing preferences are judged by this outdated method, feel there is 'nothing on television'. The digital age of accurate audience data gives the broadcasters no excuse not to serve their viewers.

License your product

A good way to product check is to check out someone else's product. Licensing a successful web presence often means that you can lock into a proven online success. This is particularly important in e-commerce, where sites appear simple on the surface but are complicated underneath, with invoice processing, inventory and e-payment systems. A good example is Amazon.com, where the site not only remembers what you have ordered in the past, but also allows you to purchase goods with one push of a button mainly because millions have been spent on its marketing and technical development.

Do not believe your in-house team of two eager 'techies' when they say that 'we can make a site which does everything that site does'. What they are actually saying is 'we can make a site which *appears* to be like that site to the casual viewer'. All the back office functions of that site, and all the systems it talks to are hidden from their gaze. It is essential to study its business model and the functions it has to fulfil. Then ask your in-house team if they can meet those demands.

That is why it is often cheaper to license from another online business, typically one in the US which would like to expand into another country.

Eloan (www.uk.eloan.com), the online mortgage selection site, launched in the UK with software which was already tried and tested in the US. Eloan Inc took a 50% stake in the UK company for the licensing of its software (and its brand). The other backers contributed start-up capital. The advantage of using the licensed software is that the US parent had already overcome such technical problems as how to calculate the monthly repayments on 1700 different mortgage products when the number of years over which the loan is paid is changed.

A newer solution is to use or adapt another company's online platform. The complexities of using the internet to source and buy from a vast number of different suppliers have produced several such platforms. They allow a company, or a coalition of companies, to create an online supply market. For example, the chemical, oil and aerospace industries have set up a common e-procurement platform, supplied by CommerceOne, a company based in Pleasanton, California.

Some commentators find it perverse that deadly rivals should combine on a common platform to buy from suppliers but this is facing electronic reality. If they compete, they will create many electronic supply standards in the industry and hold back its growth. The expense of such software is formidable and it is better that they should all shoulder the risk. Finally, it is better to have a common electronic market and compete on what they are good at (extracting and selling oil products) rather than what they are all indifferent at (creating technology).

Of course the companies which create these platforms are producing formidable markets in which many different industries use a global system to buy and sell. CommerceOne claims that it can save industries using its platform 50% of their present supply costs.

Other companies which supply common procurement platforms are Ariba, InfoBank and Baltimore. Baltimore specializes in creating highly secure centres of electronic transactions in territories with benign tax regimes.

Increasingly the strange web constructions which venture capitalists build to compete with traditional retailers are proving good hunting grounds for traditional manufacturers looking for online products and profile. For example, www.ironplanet.com was built as an electronic market for second-hand construction equipment – entirely funded by venture capital. The equipment manufacturers, Caterpillar, Volvo and Komatsu, woke up to find that their traditional dealers were competing with a very sophisticated website (also in Pleasanton, California). They decided that the best means of attack was to buy in, so they have all taken equity stakes in the IronPlanet system.

If it affects something as specialized as the construction equipment industry, it is probable that someone somewhere is funding an online system to compete with most retailers. So you can either create electronic competition or buy into the leader of the pack, probably arm in arm with your biggest competitor.

Customers are unaware of your product or its benefits

There is no point in being a brilliant entrepreneur if the public has not noticed your product. When was the last time you failed to notice a new product from Virgin? In other words, if products aren't selling, most entrepreneurs assume that people don't know about them.

The reaction to this problem is to hire a public relations company and persuade them to produce countless column inches of print coverage and interviews with the chief executive. However, this is a very one-sided approach. 'Offline' coverage (in other words, traditional media coverage) is limited by the fact that unless you have something new and interesting to say the journalists will ignore you. Their readers are not stupid, if the papers keep producing the same coverage of the same companies readers will get bored and their sales will decline.

But why rely so heavily on offline coverage? Online businesses are by definition just that – online. So the way to make people aware of your products is by using online media.

There seems to be a reluctance on the part of online enterprises to use online campaigns and deals to promote their products, despite the fact that figures consistently show such campaigns to be highly effective. Possibly online entrepreneurs cling to traditional means of promotion because they feel comfortable with them. Despite the fact that their business is all about 'creativity' their marketing is still relatively uncreative. If they have 30 seconds on television, it may be ludicrously expensive and hit only a fraction of their target audience, but at least their friends can see that they are in business.

There are much better ways to generate awareness of online products. For example, even a presence, via a link or an advertisement, on another site which is *relevant to your product* will create massive awareness.

Eloan discovered this early on. It found that deals with big internet service providers were nothing like as effective at referring business to their site as deals with sites advertising new homes. The deal with the internet service provider, where searching for information on loans or mortgages would generate a link to the Eloan site, accounted for 4.16% of visits. At the same time, Eloan had a presence on a new homes site which charges them nothing for the link, and which accounted for 42.25% of Eloan visits.

The logic is simple; catch people while they are in the mood to look at what you have to offer (for example when looking at new homes) and they will look at you. Catch them when they are thinking about something else (such as while on an internet service provider's site) and the possibility that they will visit your site declines dramatically.

The new advertising

Traditional advertising, and traditional public relations, has always had a problem – it tends to be scattergun. Tim Bell, the original chief executive of Saatchi and Saatchi, says that what has always worried him about advertising is that half of those who see your advert either don't want your product or don't like the message you are using to sell it. However, computer-based advertising will change all that. It will increase the efficiency and decrease the costs of advertising, in the same way that the internet is cutting the cost of doing business in everything from the automotive to the oil industry.

Computer-based advertising has one very important characteristic; it allows the sender to identify and talk to specific recipients. Television and newspapers cannot do this, as they have no idea which individuals will watch or read them on any given day. However, computer-based communication not only identifies who is reading your message but also allows the receiver to talk back to the advertiser.

This is set to have a big impact on public relations which is, in part, the art of influencing very small audiences who are valuable to a particular client. For example, at company results time, two important audiences should receive the story behind a company's results and they are the City editors and City analysts who cover a company. In most cases this amounts to no more than 40 people.

It would be expensive to use television or even radio advertising to reach these people and entirely possible that the chosen 40 people would never receive the message. However, it does make sense to use public relations personnel to either phone, lunch with or present to these people.

But supposing that, on the day of the results, all these influencers received an electronic communication, direct to their computer, which played them the story the company wanted them to hear, using sound and images. This new form of public relations advertising would hit the precise target audience for which it was intended, tailor the message so that it was in a form which the editors and analysts would appreciate and allow them to ask follow-up questions via the advertisement.

My company, e-communications, has been experimenting with advertisements of this sort (distributed as e-mail attachments). The software used does not require any plugs-ins or downloads to operate it (agencies accept that journalists will not go to the effort of downloading them). The attachments are small (under half a megabyte), otherwise dial-up systems will take forever to download them. e-communications has branded these public relations advertisements 'e-words'.

e-words are very interesting because of what they show about targeting and capturing the online consumer. They show that there is a real appetite among online consumers for advertisements which are very specific to them. They send a signal back to the sender when they are opened so we know that 95% of them are opened as opposed to a figure of 5% for direct mail shots. We also know that if the message is specific enough they are taken and acted upon.

Case study – DLJ Direct

Between Christmas and New Year 1999 DLJdirect Ltd, the online broker, released a number of e-words to people who had registered on their site but hadn't used it to deal in shares. Increasing the number of people actually dealing on the site was important to DLJdirect as it increased the amount of commission they earned. Analysis of the reasons people registered but didn't deal on the site showed that many people simply didn't understand what to do. An e-word was produced which explained how to deal online and was sent to all of DLJ's non-dealers.

The results were interesting: 95% of the e-words were opened and there was a 21% increase in the number of registrants dealing. The picture shows a screen from the e-word – on which a feature of DLJ's web product is shown with a text description of the benefit to the user.

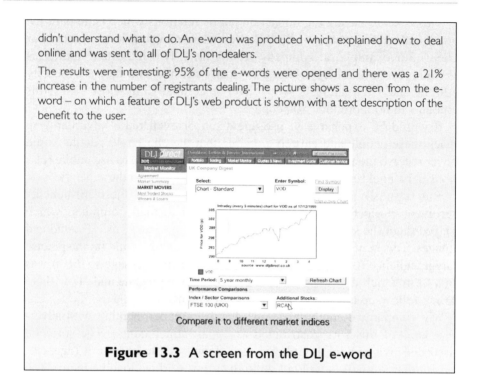

Figure 13.3 A screen from the DLJ e-word

There are less sophisticated ways in which to tackle the online audience. Many should be part of the normal process of brand building (and have been dealt with in Chapter 6).

Soon there will be many forms of online advertising, much of it sophisticated enough to note a recipient's reaction to an advertisement so that the next online advert can be tailored specifically to that individual and that individual alone. It seems a strange idea to create adverts for just one person but it is money well spent if that person's perception has a direct effect on your company's share price (for example an analyst with one of the major City fund managers). After all much of the money spent on conventional advertising is spent on reaching people who have absolutely no interest in what is being sold. Online technology will ensure that the advertisement hits that individual and that individual alone and measures his reaction to it.

The advent of online messaging puts a premium on electronic information about individuals, such as their e-mail addresses and the sites they have visited (the kind of data found in 'cookies' – see Chapter 6). These data are useful as they allow you to reach exactly the right individuals through the online media. They come from many strange sources. For example, a heavy construction equipment manufacturer wished to reach people online who were likely to be interested in buying its vehicles. It found that the lease companies, who often provide finance for equipment purchases, keep a complete electronic data file on the individuals signing their agreements and they are prepared to sell these data. In this way the equipment companies managed to purchase a database of 200,000 names in the US and are going to use them for an online advertising campaign to promote their brand.

At the moment there is no central service which tells companies wishing to run online campaigns where to buy data on individuals. But it is clearly an attractive business opportunity which anticipates the heady growth of the online advertising industry.

Supporting the brand

Your business will already have a brand position (if you have followed the method set out in Chapter 7). However, brands can be let down by their managements. For example Virgin runs a superb airline, Virgin Atlantic, which was the first to install computer games and individual movie screens in its economy class, an obvious added value. However, it also runs a train service which serves less than satisfactory food and on which it is possible to pay a full first-class fare and discover that everyone else has paid an extra £10 over economy fare for the same privileges. It makes you feel let down by the same brand. In other words, if your brand is managed badly, wherever that might be in your business, in the eyes of the customer it will erode its value.

That means that however hard one part of the business is working at reinforcing the brand, if another part of the business is underperforming, you will be wasting time and effort investing in the brand.

And so it is with the online business. The most obvious trap in online is data security. Many traditional companies are mesmerized by the need to be 'cutting edge' and offer online facilities to customers without realizing that a central component of their main brand is confidentiality and security. Immense damage was inflicted on both Barclays and British Gas when customers discovered that they could read other customers' account details via the website. The sites were not sufficiently secure and so undermined a central component of the main brand.

In checking whether your brand values could be undermined, it is useful to get away from the day-to-day running of the business and think about your brand values, even if you have already done so and even if you have paid a marketing agency to do it as well. When you are trading online it is always worth thinking about. Try and define the business's brand values by pretending that the online component in that business does not exist. This often brings out the things your business is really about, without getting lost in a haze of technology which, in truth, the consumer neither cares about nor understands.

For example, Amazon.com is a global online bookstore. To define what its brand values should be, let us imagine that it is not online at all. It is simply a very large bookstore which you can order from wherever you are. Its values might be:

1   Speed of delivery
2   The largest and most complete selection of books.

Amazon makes much of its speed of delivery. For any delivery service, whether online or offline, this makes a real difference to the consumer and is clearly part of the brand experience. Amazon has exploited this very effectively in two ways. The first is that on the day that it believes that a book will be with a customer, an e-mail is sent to him or her saying that the book will be delivered within the next 24 hours. This creates the impression that Amazon's delivery system is even faster than Amazon had realized and produces a very positive impression in the customer's mind.

The second marketing device Amazon successfully employed when it set up in London was the use of bike delivery from its new warehouse in Slough. Again it promised most books in two to three days but when an order came from a London postcode Amazon made a point of delivering the books by bike rider direct that day. Speed of delivery was then associated with Amazon in the minds of the London customers.

It is intriguing that Amazon has not made more of the second. It should be a part of its brand, and heavily promoted but instead they try for a ubiquitous presence on sites such as Yahoo! (offering a book to match the results of your search enquiry). This is impressive but is dulled by the effect of personalization where the searcher thinks 'what a coincidence, Amazon has got a book on that'. The customer does not think 'Amazon must have the *biggest collection of books available* to have a book on that', which would be good brand enhancement.

There is a third major value attached to Amazon and it is an online value. But to make it real it has to be perceived as an offline service. Amazon defeats what is perceived to be the greatest drawback of the traditional bookshop, which is that it is very difficult to find exactly what you want when you want it. People say they like to browse but the nature of the modern lifestyle means that most of us don't have time for that. An aimless meander around a shop is fast becoming a luxury few of us can afford.

But Amazon's search technology, which is some of the best on the web, allows you to find what you are looking for quickly. It is like finding the ultimate shop assistant. However, it assumes that you know how search engines work and how to narrow searches intelligently. This is an important point, as I don't think that online entrepreneurs can assume that the public is familiar with search tools and methods. They are familiar to people with an academic education, and possibly the young, but the majority of consumers, I believe, find it baffling.

Often an important factor which lets down an online brand is that online entrepreneurs do not understand the way in which consumers view or use online services. Such research as has been done on the psychology of the web[2] (which is very little) suggests that people believe that there is always another human being at the other end of a web or a search connection, when in reality most of the time they are talking to a piece of software. They feel let down by an online company when this 'human' at the other end behaves in a cold or irrational manner. Although Microsoft are great researchers into the psychology of computer use, they don't seem to have learnt much from it. For example, typically through no fault of your own, your PC will often tell you 'This programme has performed an illegal operation and will be closed down', the sort of statement one would expect from a government official who was accusing your business of polluting the neighbourhood with toxic waste. Much better is the error message carried by many mail servers now when they can't send an e-mail which reads 'I have tried for three days to send this message but I can't locate the recipient. Sorry, I have given up.' It may be slightly defeatist but at least it's polite and human.

There is a whole field of research yet to be undertaken into the psychology of how people use and perceive online services. The problem is it hasn't been done yet and if you are setting up now you will have to make your own mistakes. The simple rule is to imagine that your service is a person and say whether you would want that person to deal with one of your customers.

Some websites have cleverly got close to 'personifying' their help service to overcome the 'would you trust this site with one of your customers?' dilemma. Ask Jeeves is one, the California-based search engine (www.askjeeves.com). The group of Berkley academics who created it decided that traditional search engines were too robotic and came up with the superb marketing trick of an omniscient butler who you could ask anything in plain English. It is a meta-search engine, so it searches several search engines simultaneously, allowing its creators to concentrate on how it interacts with the fallible humans who use it.

But ask it 'Why are you called Jeeves?' and it doesn't mention P.G. Wodehouse, instead it guides you to its investor relations pages. So there is still a lot of work to be done on the relationship between humans and the internet.

Leaving your customer alone with your business

The plain fact in online is that your company is probably going to end up being represented by a computer, which presents some significant challenges about how you continue to support your brand and its values.

Some companies fudge this, for excellent reasons, and only trade online with a traditional call centre giving support. Eloan, which started online, is about to establish a call centre presence as it has discovered that people often like the reassurance of a human being. What these human beings are doing is reading off the same computer which you could be using online but handholding you. It is an expensive way of making the computer human but a highly effective one.

More ingenious solutions include what I call the 'Microsoft bug fix'. Microsoft managed to grow to the size it is today by trying to give its customers exactly the software features and functionality they required. However in doing this it has often got products to market too fast and without ironing out the bugs in them. For example, using Microsoft Express 4.0, it is often impossible to send an e-mail you are composing to the task bar, because the software won't let you.

However, Microsoft know about this and realize that they have to respond to stop their brand eroding. So rather than leave the customer saying 'Oh, that doesn't work, typical Microsoft', they give their more sophisticated users the opportunity to correct it. The Microsoft.com website is littered with areas which contain nothing but details of technical faults and how to correct them, for example www.msdn.microsoft.com/bugs, or the grandly titled 'Knowledge Base', which contains details of technical fixes and errors on all Microsoft products (www.search.support.microsoft.com/kb).

The lesson is to accept that computers (and software) are fallible and, if you are using them to support brand values, the consumer must be given a method to vent their frustration.

As the car developed from a complicated device with too many controls which only enthusiasts could operate, so too computers will develop into something which the majority can use easily.

Almost the greatest brand value you can sell online is your ease of use. It will make you different from the competition (by and large). SkyDigital spent a lot of time (even commissioning Edinburgh University to do research) on making the electronic programme guide (EPG) through which consumers access its digital services easy to operate. The constant downloading of new software on the SkyDigital system often means that the set-top boxes have to be restarted, so it invested in help lines which tell customers how to do this.

Amazon have worked very hard on ease of use. It is now possible to confirm a book order and action its delivery through a single button press on the latest version of their site.

However, the online service which is most seamless from the point of view of brand enhancement is LetsBuyIt.com (www.letsbuyit.com). This service works on the principle that the more people who get together to buy a product the more the price of the product falls. LetsBuyIt did some very colourful TV advertisements using a lot of ants to illustrate this. However, nothing is as effective as the website in showing the value of what they do. It simply shows a bar chart of a product price falling as the number of buyers increases. It is self-explanatory, easy to understand and illustrates the power of the proposition and its financial value.

Despite this brilliant piece of branding, LetsBuyIt.com did not survive the internet shake-out. It fell victim to not examining whether there was a market for mass online buying. There wasn't and it ran out of funds in January 2001.

No joins

I believe that all online businesses are capable of matching look, performance and values together so that there are no joins or contradictions. This is because online technology potentially allows customer, seller and the values of the business to sit and work together simultaneously. If you can check and define your brand values, you can pack them home with a punch never before experienced in traditional businesses.

CHECKPOINTS

- Once you have launched your online business, check your products for:

  - Utility – do they do what you say they do and are they easy to use?

  - Awareness – do your potential customers know about them?

  - Branding – are you emphasizing the correct brand values when you are promoting your business?

- Check that your online service is accessible and easy to use through:

  - Focus group testing

  - Monitoring page and customer use

  - Licensing your software from companies which have already delivered accessibility and ease of use.

- There are many ways of raising awareness of online products using online technology itself, without the expense of traditional advertising. For example:

  - Advertisements targeted at individuals and sent via e-mail

  - Linking to websites where the target audience overlaps your own.

- Constantly examine what defines your brand to your customers and whether these are the values you recognize and want to promote:

  - Often after a service is launched the values that the customer perceives change from those promoted at launch.

- Think about how to make your brand appear to be more like a person. This means making it operate so that it is:

  - Useful

  - Helpful

  - Concerned about your needs (like a good shop assistant).

CHAPTER 14

Where is It All Going?

One of the expanding sectors of the online economy is the growth industry, whose job is to predict which new online companies are going to enjoy the most rapid growth and therefore offer the best investment. The growth industry has a prodigious output. Morgan Stanley Dean Witter has a growth team who publish *The Technology Edge* which sports a cover of a bald man standing on a stool and looking over a hedge in a country lane. This is the kind of rural pastime that only international investment bankers can imagine. However, the publication is crammed with columns of useful measurements and performance indicators.

This book has so far worked on the assumption that you have an online idea and want to refine it so that it stands a chance of success. However, investment bankers believe that it is possible to spot areas of the economy which are ripe for technological reform, giving rise to the kind of online ideas in which it would be most profitable to invest.

This is a contentious area and given the rapid pace of the online revolution, you are as likely to be as right or wrong as anyone else. Most of the growth surveys seem to contain false assumptions because the growth experts have forgotten to see the world from the perspective of the customer and the benefits those customers will get from online.

For example Morgan Stanley Dean Witter state that:

The face of competition has changed following recent merger announcements of traditional and new media companies. We believe that the new credo of media CEOs should be 'Context is King, and content is important'. In our view companies that learn how to blend context and content will have higher sustainable growth rates.[1]

This is due to the belief that it is strategy (and strategic statements) which makes businesses succeed. This is only true (if it ever was) in large corporations where a chief executive is trying to develop a programme of radical change and is hoping that someone in the workforce will listen to him or her. Eighty per cent of change programmes in large corporations fail and generally generate an unpleasant series of civil wars as middle management resists the strategic changes. My advice is if you ever hear a chief executive say 'Context is King, and content is important' – is to invest your money somewhere else.

The reality of online businesses is that most of them are start-ups and must concentrate on communicating benefits to the customer. No benefits mean no customers, which in turn means no revenue, and no start-up can afford this for long.

Online markets which will grow

The online economy has only just started, and is still at the stage where most successful businesses will adapt quickly to what the consumer wants. The benefits these businesses offer will change as online matures and grows into something else. Online benefits can be defined in three broad categories:

- Providing access to information or content which was inaccessible or difficult to access before online

- Allowing consumers to buy exactly what they want when they want it (particularly true of online shopping or e-commerce)

- Radically lowering costs and increasing productivity. This is normally true of most online business to business companies.

To succeed in 2001, your online company will almost certainly have to provide at least one of these benefits.

Providing access to information or content

This has to be information which previously was difficult to access. Amazon.com is the obvious example, allowing access to (and the ability to purchase from) a vast warehouse of books. Yahoo! and Ask Jeeves.com provide a gateway to information which was unreachable before the web was created. New near video on demand systems such as BSkyB also come into this category, allowing access to movies and sporting events which were unavailable before online.

There is a debate about the implications of online service provision and how it impacts on the best place to be in the supply chain (see Chapter 2). It was believed at one point that with the spread of distribution (digital TV, broadband, video phones), the best thing to be was a content owner. That way all these new means of distribution would have to bid for your content (if it was attractive) and increase the price. This has now subtly changed to saying that 'companies able to create value in the eyes of the consumer through the use of [an online interface into the home] will prosper, but those that cannot will be unable to capture the tremendous revenue opportunity'.[2] That is to say that the *combination* of content and what can be done with it (through interactivity, video on demand or any other form of repurposing) is the thing which adds value and will spell success in the content access market.

Certainly, for those with the funds to play this game, the portal into the home will continue to be a battleground (and a growth market), both in Europe and the US. It is now possible for an online homeowner to extend a broadband feed and telephone line to the central household digital decoder and then cable out from it to distribute the resulting television pictures all over the house. A major switching centre is created behind the television cupboard in the living room. However, *any* digital box could sit in the living room and loyalty to a particular digital box is maintained by the mixture of content and interactive services which it provides (and attachment to the brand).

The fight for the gateway into the home is still in its early stages, with BSkyB, Telewest, NTL and Ondigital in the UK and TPS and Canal Plus in France.

In the US the picture is even more complicated, with a fight between satellite, cable and well-funded webcasting systems in prospect. Webcasting means delivering large amounts of content (such as video) over broadband lines on the internet. The companies best poised to take advantage of this are Clear Channel, Cox Interactive Media and Univision, and they will be taking on giants such as News Corps and the newly merged AOL Time Warner Inc. You need deep pockets to enter this market and that will put off many start-ups. However, Morgan Stanley Dean Witter expects penetration of expanded digital television services to leap from 20% of households in 2000 to 50% by 2005.[1]

Allowing consumers to buy exactly what they want when they want it

I see this as the holy grail (and huge growth market) of the second wave of online services. Although we know that this is part of the very essence of the online consumer (see Chapter 1), still very few applications have managed to deliver it successfully. Much of the success of Napster.com (the online music download service) can be attributed to delivering exactly what consumers want when they want it. However, other examples remain scarce.

I think allowing consumers to buy exactly what they want when they want it is, in many ways, the kind of killer application which broadband access to the internet will deliver. Current internet access rates are easily affordable at 56 kilobits/sec but this doesn't allow you to watch anything but small and jumpy video pictures and causes big problems for any download over about 2 megabits (which can take about ten minutes). It is possible to purchase a 512 kb/sec internet connection for £30 a month, but this still doesn't really give television quality video although downloading is much easier.

However, at 2 meg/sec video is completely viable and this is what is being offered by telephone exchanges in the UK once they have upgraded to the ADSL technology. I believe that at this level (once it is affordable) the online revolution really does enter its second stage, because at that speed all kinds of content can be viewed by the consumer exactly when he or she wants it, without any appreciable wait.

At this point the household digital box will form an on demand centre in the middle of the household from which information, video, audio and interactive content will be accessed at the whim of any user in the house. This will create a clear and permanent connection between online content providers and the consumer.

It is hard to imagine all the services which will grow out of this step change. However, one is emerging now which is easy to see and that is interactive learning.

The online society will have to develop interactive learning, because in a society in which skills rapidly become obsolete there has to be an engine for renewing them. Traditional education finds it hard to update learning material quickly enough to keep pace with any kind of social change – let alone online change – so electronically updated learning and learning material is the answer.

Marjorie Scardino, chief executive of Pearson plc, has already moved the company in this direction by disposing of the television production division and buying heavily into learning companies, both in Europe and

---

USA 2001: the killer application

Online learning is, according to John Chambers, the CEO of Cisco Systems, the 'killer app' of the internet. In the US, serious companies are investing quickly and heavily in order to grab market share in a new internet gold rush.

Michael Milken, the former junk bond king, runs Knowledge Universe, an online company incubator and investor which only backs educational and training companies. The *Washington Post* is also involved in online education, including KaplanCollege.com which offers 500 online courses across nine professions. Twenty million dollars has been invested to launch Global Education Network which will offer online courses from some of America's top colleges including Brown, Wellesley and Williams.

There are good reasons for backing online education. At present what students, on technical university courses, such as those for computing or engineering, learn in their first year is out of date by the time they graduate. This inevitably leads to lifelong learning where students will have to have their education constantly updated. Online is clearly an attractive way of doing this, not merely because it can be achieved quickly but because it is cheap. For the average company, using e-learning is 50–90% cheaper than bringing in real-life teachers and holding formal classes.

The companies making the running for now in the USA are, as ever, the applications providers. They provide software that companies can use to design and create online coursework. Two market leaders are Smartforce and DigitalThink. At the end of 1999 Smartforce signed a $25 million deal with Unisys. DigitalThink has similar deals with Cisco, Charles Schwab and Deutsche Bank.

However, any learning is only as good as the teaching and the content and that is where the big challenge now lies. The two main issues are creating content which is fully interactive, and this is harder than writing conventional content as the material has to be capable of being accessed in many different ways. Eli Noam, of Columbia Business School says that, 'It is vastly harder than preparing a classroom course, 20 times the effort'.[3] The second issue is making the software appear to provide the intelligence and sympathy of a teacher. 'People tend to lose interest if there's nobody on the other side who cares if I'm here or not',[3] says Vicky Phillips of GetEducated.com. That is where the challenge for the first wave of online education entrepreneurs lies.

---

the US. Microsoft has been in the market for some time as it had to provide online learning in order to create a large enough skills base for the installation and training which its products required. Traditional players such as the UK's City and Guilds currently have a whole range of online learning services under development.

Radically lowering costs and increasing productivity

This is the territory dominated by business to business applications. Business to consumer costs are harder to quantify, however, it is worth reflecting that there are radical changes to an individual's productivity as a result of online. For example, it is now quicker and easier to get information on holidays and technology problems, and to get your business and presentational material to companies. To this the cynic says: 'yes, but what about technical breakdowns, bugs and viruses?' Despite this, individuals are able to do more from the office, home, or laptop. It is having a profound effect on the productivity of idea creators and sellers, such as consultants. Some of the implications of this are examined later.

But the quantifiable cost decreases have already occurred where there are lots of sellers and very big buyers. This is the market occupied by Ariba.com and CommerceOne.com, who have created global electronic marketplaces, using the web, for industries (such as energy and aerospace) and for groups of companies in definable areas (such as France and Italy).

Groups of large companies (for example oil) seem to have swallowed the idea that creating a large electronic market of all their suppliers and pooling it with their competitors is a good idea, because they all enjoy the same cost reductions. The obvious flaw in this is that apparently it gives none of them a competitive advantage in their marketplace. However, it has driven a tremendous growth in e-procurement platform providers. I think that growth will now translate into the next wave of online commerce development and that is e-payments.

E-commerce will always be held back until a viable online payment system has developed, because traditional payment systems are expensive. Even credit cards contain high transactions costs compared to the costs involved in transmitting and receiving e-money (Figure 14.1).

There is a huge growth opportunity involved in developing e-payment systems, particularly for B2C companies. The companies most likely to develop it are, I believe, telecommunications companies (particularly mobile phone operators) and the e-procurement platforms. This is because both of these types of business are being held back by a lack of e-payment systems. The banks, I believe, will not be leaders in this field as they are making the large margins on the traditional payment methods. However, there will clearly be opportunities for entrepreneurs with technological expertise who would like to partner telecom companies or perhaps even banks.

The other growth area for lowering costs and boosting productivity is online security operations. The reason for this is that the humble e-mail still lacks various features which the letter jealously guards, namely legal status and a signature. The two are very important as it is, for example, possible to borrow large sums of money using signed letters in the conventional post.

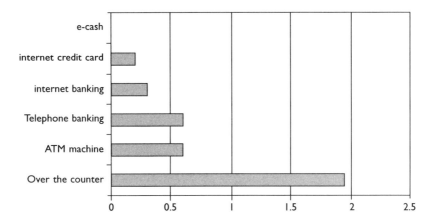

Figure 14.1 Costs of transferring money into cash using several different means of transmission

The e-mail can possess this but it requires parties to have digital signatures and normally encryption. Microsoft (and others) is trying to create standards in this area but has not marketed it well. In the B2B area, Baltimore.com is doing much better. However, there is huge growth in this whole area and a market leader has yet to emerge.

Subtle changes

All books on this subject talk about 'revolution' and 'shocks'. However, I think some of the most exciting developments in the way in which online affects us will be gradual and will come upon us imperceptibly. There are certainly opportunities for employment in them and also opportunities for entrepreneurs. However, the important factor will be to get the timing correct as gradual change means that markets take time to develop.

Three particular areas for future development are now discussed.

Employment

There should be a gradual change in both the way in which people work and the means by which they find a job in the first place.

One of the liberating forces behind online is that it is hard to be successful unless your employees are well rewarded, motivated and have responsibility and the scope to experiment. This is not to say they will be undisciplined, as projects can only be achieved through goals and application. However work as a whole should become more rewarding, both mentally and financially.

Much of this work will be pure ideas – how to run businesses, how the world will develop and how to grow the world. What has been the realm of academics and management gurus will become the everyday work of knowledge workers. And that work will be highly dependent on online technology for communication, research and, most importantly, modelling the behaviour of an organization or environment.

It could be argued that all this is already with us. But in a way it isn't, as ideas people often work in rather unresponsive, large organizations which limit the scope of what is done and how. As the ideas industry progresses, I believe that consultants increasingly will be called on to create new methods for dealing with rapidly changing industrial environments so that models of how to conduct business and new marketplaces will become the substance of idea work. It is possible to imagine whole new ways of doing business in which the inventor has a commission on every transaction and retires at 40 on the proceeds, rather in the way that pop stars do at present.

This way of working is only possible under online as the technology allows a global account to be kept of all transactions in a market and informs the inventor at home where those transactions are taking place.

It should be easier to find a new job. I believe that this is the real test of the online economy. If online can deliver a perfect and comprehensive flow of information globally, it should be easy for it to deliver the ideal job after a minimal search, and not the six-months average that headhunters tell people it takes to find a new job at the moment. This makes job and employment sites very interesting territory. However, at the moment, these sites are not impressive as they are too conventional, simply being a transposition of the appointments section of a traditional newspaper to web pages. Take a look at www.stepstone.com, for example.

Perhaps this is an area which requires a high degree of interactivity and personalization so that candidates get the impression a job is being built up for them. It may not be available that day, but an online presence with a high volume of vacancies would be able to alert a job seeker when something approaching his or her skills set and passions appeared.

However, I think this is probably an area where consumer perceptions and demand ('it is my right to have a fulfilling job and this technology should provide it') are behind the way I believe that this market will develop. It is entirely consistent with 'exactly what I want when I want it'.

Capital

There has been a subtle change in the funding of online businesses. One chairman said to me that he was amazed at the stunned silence that greeted him when he enquired whether entrepreneurs, who had come to him for capital, were going to put any of their own money into the proposed business. It is almost expected now that entrepreneurs can raise capital without mortgaging their own home. All they have to do is submit a business plan and hope someone somewhere has money to invest.

There is much money to be invested, essentially because the western world is affluent. But it is mainly because investors, due to computers, have got better at calculating acceptable degrees of risk. In the end it all comes back to ideas and computer modelling.

However the online boom showed that there were difficulties matching investors with the kind of ideas with which they felt comfortable. I therefore think there will be more electronic markets matching online ideas with potential investors and management talent. Such things have been tried in the past but have failed to produce tangible results. Perhaps it awaits the personalization of electronic job seeking to make it really fly.

Advertising

Advertising and the communication of commercial messages will be profoundly affected by online. The major sea change is in the ability of the computer to send a message intended for a single individual. This means that it is now possible to advertise to very small groups of individuals and form an electronic relationship with them.

However the advertising industry and its clients have been slow to adopt this. The historic power of television is too ingrained in their psyche for them to believe that television advertising is on the wane. But it is – all major TV channels have declining audiences and, judging by Christmas viewing figures in the UK, children now prefer playing with interactive games to watching TV.

However advertising will change as the amount of time spent on online devices increases and the users of those online devices demand that media is more specific to them and less targeted at a mass audience. It is a challenge to which advertisers have barely risen.

Subtle, strange and immeasurable

The most peculiar industry which the unstoppable march of the quicksilver companies has spawned is the study of deflation. There is a fundamental economic reason why governments worldwide want to encourage entrepreneurs to enter the online battleground and that is because it kills inflation. Inflation was the scourge of the post-war world. It eroded pensions, produced irresistible wage demands, led to price hikes and was the handmaiden of falling living standards.

However, with the personal computer revolution, then the telecommunications revolution and finally with online, Europe and America have reduced inflation. Online and computers now mean that an individual's ability to produce goods and services has been boosted so much that inflation is falling. In other words, the net effect of online is deflation.

The problem is no one is quite sure how to measure this effect. But this deflation is already built into US economic statistics. Productivity increases from online also boost the wealth a nation is producing (its GDP). It has been estimated that the productivity increases due to computers and information technology in the US economy presently increase the US GDP by 1% – a massive amount. So far little work has been done on the resultant increases in productivity in the service sector, although US statisticians are now working on this. However, the increase in the wealth of the western world is bigger than thought and probably increasing faster than thought. This leads to several ideas, which I believe the quicksilver entrepreneur should have uppermost in his or her mind.

First, in setting up a quicksilver company you ought to do your best, if only for yourself and this book is an attempt to give you a set of disciplines to do that.

Second, in doing so you are making everyone wealthier, as online industry kills inflation and boosts productivity and is the ultimate prescription for old, inflation-ridden economies. We are never going back there. Not after online.

Third, if you make a lot of money please donate some to the establishment of an Institute for the Study of Deflation as there is an urgent need to quantify the true, beneficial effects of the online revolution.

And finally, never listen to those who say that online is a temporary phenomenon which will go away as did tulip mania in 17th-century Holland. Online is about both building and seeing a much better future.

Having seen the online future, it is impossible to forget it. That is why it will continue like quicksilver, fast, treacherous, alluring and glittering with new wealth.

Chapter 1

1   *Sunday Times Business Section*, 29 October 2000.
2   All quoted at www.henleycentre.com.
3   Quoted in *Richard Branson* by Mick Brown, Headline, London, New York, Japan, 1998, p. 463.

Chapter 2

1   Cephren was the master builder responsible for the Pyramids, according to these Californian dot.commers.

Chapter 3

1   Alan Turing, the British academic who created the world's first computer at Manchester University, defined 'artificial intelligence' as the state in which someone cannot tell if a computer's responses come from the computer itself or a human manipulating it.
2   *Financial Times*, 28 November 2000.
3   *Financial Times*, 15 August 2000. Inside Track by Tim Jackson.

Chapter 5

1   Compeer research, quoted in *Financial Times*, 20 November 2000.

Chapter 7

1   *Competitive Advantage*, Michael E. Porter, Free Press, New York, 1985, p. 9.

Chapter 8

1   'Paper' meaning 'shares' in this context. City people have an unsentimental sense of humour which normally involves laughing at others' misfortunes – knowing that, but for the grace of God, it could have been them.

2   From an article in the *Sunday Times*, 17 September 2000.
3   *Financial Times*, 18 July 2000.
4   *Accounting for Growth – Stripping the Camouflage from Company Accounts*, Terry Smith, Random House, London, New York, Japan, 1992.

Chapter 9

1   Esther is a Californian internet venture capitalist, guru and allegedly a millionaire. She had heard about our parties from the internet, so dropped in.

Chapter 10

1   *Internet Business*, November 2000, p. 134.
2   UK Treasury response reported in *Internet Business*, November 2000, p. 134.
3   As long as it will return profits of more than £300,000 – as there is small companies tax rate of 20% in the UK.

Chapter 11

1   Professor of Business Administration at Harvard Business School and author of *The Change Masters*.
2   This seems to be based on the American expression 'on the road to Abilene' which means 'all going mad together'. It is probably based on the fact that Abilene was the destination for cattle being driven up from Texas on their way to be rail freighted to the slaughter houses of Chicago.
3   For a fuller account of Belbin see Charles Handy, *Understanding Organisations*, Penguin, London, New York, Japan, 4th edn 1993, pp. 160–1.

Chapter 12

1   *Business Policy*, Luffman, Sanderson, Lea and Kenny, Blackwell 1991, p. 7.
2   *Campaign*, 19 December 2000.

Chapter 13

1   Focus group research companies claim that if you put men and women together the women will not say what they really think.
2   Microsoft research.

Chapter 14

1   *From the Technology Edge*, Global Media Team, Morgan Stanley Dean Witter, London, New York, Japan, 18 October 2000.
2   *Broadband Big Bang and Aftershocks*, Global Media Team, Morgan Stanley Dean Witter, London, New York, Japan, 27 October 2000.
3   Noam and Phillips both quoted in The Virtual Classroom v. The Real One, Forbes.com, 19 November 2000.